The Pocket Encyclopedia of World Aircraft in Color

BOMBERS

BETWEEN THE WARS
1919–39

The Pocket Encyclopedia
of World Aircraft in Color

BOMBERS

BETWEEN THE WARS

1919–39

Including Patrol and Transport Aircraft

by
KENNETH MUNSON

Illustrated by
JOHN W. WOOD

Norman Dinnage
Frank Friend
Brian Hiley
William Hobson
Tony Mitchell
Jack Pelling

THE MACMILLAN COMPANY

First American Edition 1970
First published in Great Britain in 1970 by
Blandford Press Ltd., London

Library of Congress Catalog Card Number 74–124872

THE MACMILLAN COMPANY
866 Third Avenue, New York, NY 10022

Color printed by the Ysel Press, Deventer, Holland
Text printed and books bound in England
by Richard Clay (The Chaucer Press), Ltd.,
Bungay, Suffolk

PREFACE

The so-called 'years between the wars' – during which the world was never free from internal or international strife in one quarter or another – were perhaps the most colourful years in the short history of aviation, in every sense of the word. Progress in aeroplane design and performance was, predictably, slower than it had been under the impetus of a major war, yet these twenty years bridged the gap between the wood-and-fabric biplanes of 1914–18 and the metal-skinned monoplanes of 1939–45. A selection of seventy bomber aircraft typical of the period appears in the pages which follow. Flying boats falling into the categories covered by this volume will be dealt with separately in due course.

Once again our thanks go to Ian D. Huntley, whose extensive researches into aircraft colours and markings continue to be the foundation upon which the colour plates are based. Special thanks are also due to Mr W. B. Klepacki, for much valuable advice and practical assistance with several of the French and Eastern European aircraft portrayed; and to Mr E. Sekigawa for similar kindnesses in connection with the Japanese entries.

Grateful acknowledgement is also made of items published at various times by *The Aeromodeller*, *Air Classics*, *Air Pictorial*, *Aviation Magazine International*, the *Journal of the American Aviation Historical Society*, *Flying Review International*, the British and French *IPMS Magazines* and Profile Publications Ltd. Finally, my thanks are extended to Miss Edwina Bewkey for so kindly undertaking the typing of the manuscript.

Kenneth Munson

May 1970

INTRODUCTION

The creation of the Royal Air Force on 1 April 1918 brought into being the world's first fully autonomous air service, answerable to neither Army nor Navy. It was followed only a few weeks later by the formation of an Independent Force, whose entire *raison d'être* was to carry out the sustained bombing of German military and industrial targets. Five of its squadrons were made up of single-engined day bombers, but the other four squadrons were equipped with the twin-engined Handley Page O/100 and O/400 night bombers. This force, commanded by Major-General Sir Hugh Trenchard, was the first in the world to be created as a specialised long range strategic bombing force, and played a valuable role in the closing months of World War 1.

With the drastic reduction in the size of the RAF that followed the Armistice of November 1918, Trenchard was reappointed to his former post as Chief of the Air Staff with the task of reorganising an efficient service around the 33 combat squadrons that remained out of the 188 possessed by the RAF when the war ended. Of the Independent Force, Trenchard said: 'The necessities of war created it in a night, but the economies of peace have to a large extent caused it to wither in a day, and we are now faced with the necessity of replacing it with a plant of deeper root'. The 10-year rule for Imperial Defence, based on the assumption that no new major war would break out during that period, resulted in small post-war budgets that included no money for new types of aircraft: the best of those in being in 1918 would have to suffice at least for the first few years of the new-found peace.

Thus the hard core of the early post-war bomber force consisted of the single-engined D.H.9A, the twin-engined D.H.10 (which had barely begun to enter service before the Armistice) and the larger Vickers Vimy, which took the place of the Handley Pages. When it became obvious that 'the war to end wars' had done nothing of the kind, there was soon plenty of work for these and other RAF aircraft to do, in the Middle East, India and elsewhere.

The development of bomber aircraft that could attack targets great distances from home had reached a point by November 1918 where Handley Page V/1500's were standing by to carry a 1,000 lb (454 kg) load of bombs each to Berlin. As if to emphasise the long-distance capabilities of large multi-engined aeroplanes, the Vickers Vimy figured in a number of dramatic flights during 1919, the first and greatest of which was the non-stop crossing of the North Atlantic by Captain John Alcock and Lieutenant Arthur Whitten-Brown in June – a remarkable achievement by the men, the aeroplane, and the Rolls-Royce Eagle engines that powered it. The excellence of this 12-cylinder liquid-cooled Vee-type engine proved to be some consolation for the dismal failure of the ABC Dragonfly radial engine upon which so many of Britain's post-war fighter hopes had been laid.

France, whose *Aviation Militaire* was the largest and best-equipped air force in Europe at the time of the Armistice, reduced her air force to some 180 squadrons, and nearly 40 of these were equipped with bomber aircraft, mostly Breguet 14's and 16's at first and later with Breguet 19's. France, like Britain, found it necessary to deploy a large proportion of her air force on peace-keeping duties in her overseas territories.

The Italian Air Force also suffered a quick and drastic reduction from its November 1918 strength of nearly 1,800 aircraft, but was re-created as an autonomous service in 1923 after the accession to power of Benito Mussolini, and subsequently expanded with comparative rapidity to become one of the largest air forces in Europe. The Russian air force and aircraft industry had inevitably suffered serious setbacks from the 1917 Revolution, and the new Soviet air force did not begin to place itself on a firm footing until 1924.

A separate Air Service of the United States Army was created from the former Signal Corps organisation in April 1918, but for virtually the whole period of her involvement in World War 1 America had drawn her combat aircraft from European sources, the home industry manufacturing mostly training aircraft. By the Armistice plans were well advanced for the extensive licence production in the US of several European types, including Handley Page and Italian Caproni heavy bombers, but contracts

8

for these were curtailed immediately the war ended in favour of the development of aircraft of domestic origin, and the only foreign aircraft to be built in substantial numbers was the British D.H.4 single-engined day bomber. At the beginning of 1919 it was planned to have a post-war Army Air Service of some 24,000 officers and men and a little over 5,000 aircraft; but a year later Congress cut the proposed military aviation budget by two-thirds, and the funds which it did approve contained no allowance at all for new aircraft. The size of the Air Service was cut to 27 squadrons, instead of the 87 that had been planned; only four of these were bomber squadrons, and only one of them had Martin MB-2 heavy bombers.

This excessively modest-sized air force, for one of the largest nations in the world, was adhered to for several years in spite of fierce attempts by many Americans to demonstrate the need, not only for a larger force, but for one that was independent of the other US Services, following the example set by the RAF. The leading voice in this campaign was that of Colonel William Mitchell, whose championship of his beliefs ultimately cost him his career. In July 1921 Mitchell persuaded the US Army and Navy to stage mock attacks against a number of captured German warships in Chesapeake Bay, using the MB-2 and O/400 'heavies' – and even DH-4B's with 100 lb (45 kg) bombs. Three of the German ships, including the supposedly unsinkable battleship *Ostfriesland*, were sent to the bottom. But in spite of this proof, and Mitchell's continued advocacy of the value of air power (and of strategic bombing in particular), out of a total of nearly 1,400 aircraft on strength in the summer of 1924 only 59 were bombers. In the following year Mitchell's unrelenting outspokenness on the subject of air power brought him a court-martial and dismissal from the Service. The truth of his arguments was not admitted officially until many years later, after his death, when he was posthumously 'reinstated' with the USAAF rank of General. The B-25 medium bomber of World War 2 was named after him.

America, like Britain, pinned many of her post-war hopes upon a single type of aero-engine, one that first appeared during the late war. This was the 400 hp 12-cylinder Vee-type Liberty engine, over-publicised when it first appeared as the 'perfected' aero-engine when it was a long way from being perfect. But once it had undergone normal and thorough development it became the staple powerplant of many early post-war American aircraft until the arrival of the first successful radials such as the Wasp and Whirlwind.

Thus it was not until some four or five years after the end of World War 1 that really viable types of new combat aircraft began to make their appearance, and they included designs originating in countries still relatively new to the military aviation scene, such as Czechoslovakia, Japan, the Netherlands and Poland. The middle 1920s also saw the first signs of a new breakthrough in the materials of construction, even though the aircraft were still based largely upon concepts evolved during the recent war. The Dutchman Anthony Fokker was among the first to build airframes made of welded steel tube instead of the more traditional wooden construction, and the scarcity of suitable timber coupled with the extra lightness and greater strength of metal tubes or strips brought about an increasing use of metal in construction as the years went by. For some time, plywood and fabric continued to be the main covering materials, but as early as 1920 the British firm of Short Brothers had pointed the way to future trends with an ambitious and far-seeing design called the Silver Streak, which had its wings and fuselage covered with a stressed skin made of duralumin.

The general use of metal skinning appeared on bomber aircraft somewhat earlier than on fighters, due largely to the pioneering work of Junkers and another German engineer, Dr Adolph Rohrbach. The latter realised that the traditional Junkers method of using corrugated metal skins resulted in strength, but at the same time created considerable drag which affected the aeroplane's performance. He therefore took the process a stage further by developing smooth metal skins. His ideas were incorporated in two British designs, the huge Beardmore Inflexible experimental bomber and the Fairey Long Range Monoplane, but did not gain immediate general acceptance; metal skins for aircraft did not become general until the 1930s.

An important trend-setting design in this respect was the Boeing B-9 bomber which appeared in 1931. In addition to being built entirely of metal, it was a cantilever low-wing monoplane, carried its 2,260 lb (1,025 kg) bomb load entirely enclosed within its semi-monocoque fuselage, and had a retractable undercarriage

– a feature first employed on the Dayton-Wright RB racing monoplane 11 years before and only now introduced on a major combat aeroplane. Only a trial batch of seven B-9's were built, but the advanced features which this aeroplane displayed heralded a trend to be followed quickly both in the US and elsewhere. A year later the new bomber 'image' was consolidated in the handsome Martin B-10, and soon other countries began to produce designs based upon similar principles – Germany's Heinkel He 70, the Soviet SB-2, Japan's G3M, and Britain's Blenheim were among the first examples. Only France seemed reluctant to follow the new trend, and continued to turn out a succession of ugly, angular monstrosities for several more years; but when French designers did at last begin to follow suit their products, such as the Bre 690 and LeO 45, were among the most elegant of all. Nor was the influence of the B-9 confined to the military sphere, for Boeing's twin-engined Model 247 airliner, which appeared in 1932, sparked off the same revolution in commercial transport design and led to the Douglas DC-3 and Lockheed Electra.

Meanwhile, other new techniques were contributing towards improved aircraft performance. One was the Handley Page 'slotted' wing, in which a curved slat projected from the leading-edge of the main wing, forcing air through the gap between the two surfaces and over the upper surface of the wing. This helped to reduce turbulence at large angles of attack by smoothing out the airflow over the top of the wing, and so postponed the point at which the wing stalled. In 1928 the Air Ministry made it mandatory for all aircraft of the British Services to be fitted with leading-edge slots.

The use of metal was extended to propeller manufacture in the 1920s, and when practical propeller designs offering first variable pitch and then constant speed made their appearance during the first half of the 1930s this vital part of the aeroplane was at last enabled to extract the maximum possible performance out of both engine and airframe. Coupled with the improvements made in the performance of aero-engines, and of radial engines in particular, aircraft were able to fly both faster and higher. In 1933 Bristol Pegasus radial engines enabled the Westland Wallace and P.V.3 to fly over the summit of the world's highest mountain. By the outbreak of World War 2 the world absolute height record stood at 56,046 ft (17,083 m), reached by the Caproni Ca 161*bis* on the power of a single 700 hp Piaggio P.XI RC 100 radial engine; and another Pegasus-engined aircraft, the Vickers Wellesley, held the world non-stop distance record at 7,162 miles (11,526 km).

The concept of the long range strategic bomber took another important step forward when the appearance of modern large four-engined types brought a new meaning to the adjective 'heavy' and relegated earlier generations of twin-engined bombers to the medium category. Such bombers were not new – Russia had used the four-engined *Ilya Mourometz* as early as 1915, and the huge Tupolev TB-3 in the early 1930s followed in the same tradition. But the Boeing B-17 Fortress ushered in the era of the cantilever low-wing monoplane to this class of bomber.

In a general sense it is true to say that the development of military aviation proceeds at a more leisurely pace in times of peace than it does in wartime, for financial reasons if for no other. And, in the main, the minor colonial conflicts, tribal uprisings and lesser international incidents which engaged the world's air forces between 1919 and 1939 could be coped with satisfactorily by the existing types of warplane already in service. For example, in the autumn of 1935 Italy encountered little serious air opposition when it decided to add Ethiopia to its collection of East African territories. But in the summer of the following year a civil war broke out in Spain when General Francisco Franco Bahamonde led a Nationalist uprising against the reigning Republican government. Domestic though this war may have been in its origins, it very quickly became an international arena, to which France, Germany, Italy, Czechoslovakia and Russia all openly sent support to one side or the other according to their political sympathies, while arms, equipment and mercenaries from these and other countries became embroiled in the conflict in a less direct or 'official' manner.

This wholesale foreign intervention in what was essentially an internal struggle may not in all cases have been for purely ideological reasons, but one thing was certain: the war in Spain was seen as a splendid opportunity to try out warplanes both old and new, and their crews, under genuine combat conditions. The war lasted for nearly three years, finally coming to an end on 29 March 1939, and there is no doubt that, for the major nations involved, it did provide a vast amount of experience that was built into later generations of combat aircraft. On the other hand the technical and numerical superiority of, particularly, the German and Italian aircraft involved over their inferior opponents painted a somewhat exaggerated picture of their capabilities, leading to the belief that they could overcome any opposition with comparable impunity. This belief was to receive a rude awakening only a year or two later.

On the other side of the globe another international situation reached breaking point in the summer of 1937, when the long-standing quarrel between Japan and China flared into open warfare, also involving the air force of Soviet Russia in the northern territories of Mongolia and Manchuria. In August 1937 the Soviet and Chinese Nationalist governments entered into a mutual non-aggression pact, but their united resistance to the Japanese invasion of China was in the end unsuccessful.

Japan, whose domestic aircraft industry had been built up steadily after the impetus of the visit by an Air Mission from Britain in 1921, now had indisputably the most modern and powerful air force in south-east Asia, including a substantial fleet of carrier-based aircraft. But already, in Europe, an even larger and more militant power was threatening world peace.

By devious means, Germany had been skirting the prohibitions of the 1919 Versailles Treaty ever since the middle 1920s, and when Adolf Hitler's National Socialist party came to power in 1933 one of its first actions was to speed up the establishment of a powerful new air force, the *Luftwaffe*, whose existence was admitted openly two years later with the appointment of Hermann Goering, the former Air Minister, as its first Commander-in-Chief. In a speech on 8 March 1935, Goering declared: 'The lines of my policy have not been to create an offensive air arm which might constitute a threat to other nations, but to provide Germany with a military air force strong enough to defend her at any time against aerial attack'. Exactly what was the defensive purpose of such aircraft as the Junkers Ju 87 dive-bomber, whose design had been initiated some two years previously, the *Reichsmarschall* conveniently omitted to explain.

In 1935 it might perhaps have seemed that the *Luftwaffe* was comparable to, but not necessarily superior than, other major world air forces. But by the end of 1936 the end of the service life of many of the interim crop of combat aircraft was in sight, for the more significant 'second generation' bombers such as the Dornier Do 17 and Heinkel He 111 had begun to enter service.

The threat to world peace of a militant Germany was seen by some as an actual one, by others only as a potential one; but in either case the very existence of this obviously powerful new force could not be ignored, and the other major aeronautical powers began, with varying degrees of urgency, to expand and rearm their own air services with more modern types of aircraft. The Munich agreement of September 1938 was, on a political level, an act of appeasement towards a power-hungry dictator. But the rearmament of most nations, even by 1939, had by no means caught up with the resources of the Nazi war machine. Had World War 2 broken out in September 1938, instead of twelve months later, who can say what turn events might have taken?

THE COLOR PLATES

As an aid to identification, the color plates which follow have been arranged in an essentially visual order, within the broad sequence: single-engined biplanes, multi-engined biplanes, single-engined monoplanes, multi-engined monoplanes and single-engined amphibians. The reference number of each type corresponds to the appropriate text matter, and an index to all types illustrated appears on pp. 164–165.

The 'split' plan view, adopted to give both upper and lower surface markings within a single plan outline, depicts the color scheme appearing above and below either the port or starboard half of the aircraft, according to whichever aspect is shown in the side elevation.

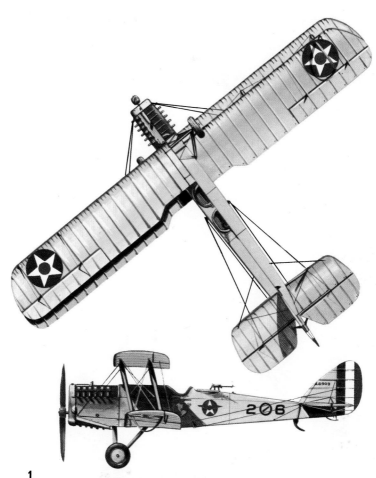

1

Boeing O2B-1 (DH-4M-1) of the US Marine Corps, *ca* 1927. *Engine:* One 416 hp V-1650 Liberty 12A 12-cylinder Vee type *Span:* 42 ft 5 in. (12·93 m). *Length:* 29 ft 11 in. (9·12 m). *Height:* 9 ft 8 in. (2·95 m). *Take-off weight:* 4,510 lb (2,046 kg). *Maximum speed:* 118 mph (190 km/hr) at sea level. *Operational ceiling:* 12,800 ft (3,902 m). *Range:* 330 miles (531 km). *Armament:* One 0·30 in. machine-gun in rear cockpit.

LETOV Sm-1 (Czechoslovakia)

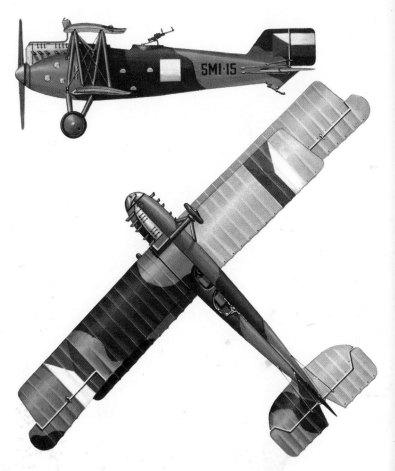

2

Letov Sm-1 (SH 1) of the Czechoslovak Air Force, *ca* 1921–22. *Engine:* One 230 hp Hiero L 6-cylinder in-line. *Span:* 43 ft 3¾ in. (13·20 m). *Length:* 27 ft 2¾ in. (8·30 m). *Height:* 10 ft 2 in. (3·10 m). *Take-off weight:* 3,031 lb (1,375 kg). *Maximum speed:* 121 mph (194 km/hr) at 6,562 ft (2,000 m). *Operational ceiling:* 19,685 ft (6,000 m). *Range:* 444 miles (715 km). *Armament:* Two 7·7 mm machine-guns, one in upper front fuselage and one in rear cockpit; up to 265 lb (120 kg) of bombs beneath lower wings.

3

Aero A 11 (possibly an aircraft of the 1st Air Regiment), Czechoslovak Air Force, 1923. *Engine:* One 240 hp Walter W-IV 8-cylinder Vee type. *Span:* 41 ft 11¼ in. (12·78 m). *Length:* 26 ft 10¾ in. (8·20 m). *Height:* 10 ft 2 in. (3.10 m). *Take-off weight:* 3,265 lb (1,481 kg). *Maximum speed:* 134 mph (215 km/hr) at 8,202 ft (2,500 m). *Operational ceiling:* 23,622 ft (7,200 m). *Range:* 466 miles (750 km). *Armament:* One 7·7 mm machine-gun in rear cockpit.

POLIKARPOV R-5 (U.S.S.R.)

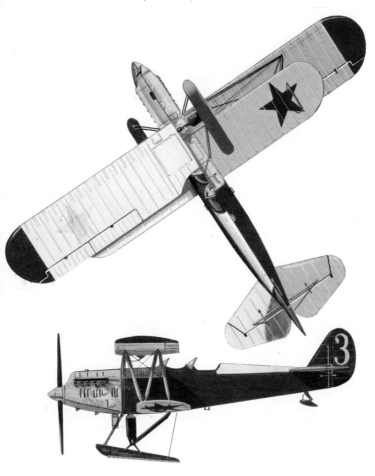

4

Polikarpov R-5 of the Soviet Air Force, *ca* 1931–32. *Engine:* One 680 hp M-17 12-cylinder Vee type. *Span:* 50 ft 10¼ in. (15·50 m). *Length:* 34 ft 7½ in. (10,555 m). *Height:* 10 ft 8 in. (3·25 m). *Take-off weight:* 6,515 lb (2,955 kg). *Maximum speed:* 142 mph (228 km/hr) at 9,843 ft (3,000 m). *Operational ceiling:* 20,997 ft (6,400 m). *Range:* 497 miles (800 km). *Armament:* One 7·62 mm PV-1 machine-gun on port side of upper front fuselage and one 7·62 mm DA-1 gun in rear cockpit; up to eight 44 or 66 lb (20 or 30 kg) bombs beneath lower wings.

BREGUET XIX (France)

5
Breguet XIX B.2 of an Army Group of the EPA (Greek National War Aviation forces), *ca* 1930. *Engine:* One 500 hp Hispano-Suiza 12 Hb 12-cylinder Vee type. *Span:* 48 ft 7¾ in. (14·83 m). *Length:* 31 ft 2 in. (9·50 m). *Height:* 10 ft 11½ in. (3·34 m). *Normal take-off weight:* 4,850 lb (2,200 kg). *Maximum speed:* 143 mph (230 km/hr) at 9,843 ft (3,000 m). *Operational ceiling:* 21,982 ft (6,700 m). *Maximum range:* 497 miles (800 km). *Armament:* One 7·5 mm Darne or 7·7 mm Vickers machine-gun in upper front fuselage, one or two similar guns in rear cockpit and one mounted ventrally to fire rearward; up to 970 lb (440 kg) of bombs beneath lower wings and fuselage.

KAWASAKI ARMY TYPE 88 (Japan)

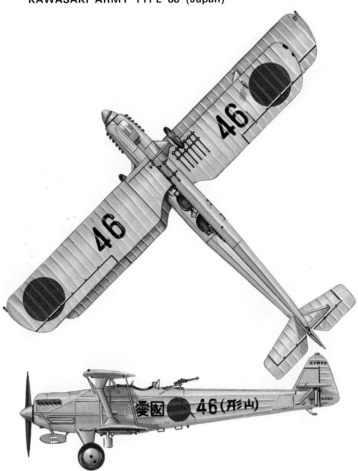

6

Kawasaki Army Type 88 bomber in markings denoting donation to the JAAF, *ca* 1929–30. *Engine:* One 500 hp Kawasaki-built BMW VI 12-cylinder Vee type. *Span:* 49 ft 10½ in. (15·20 m). *Length:* 40 ft 3½ in. (12·28 m). *Height:* 11 ft 1¾ in. (3·40 m). *Take-off weight:* 6,834 lb (3,100 kg). *Maximum speed:* 130 mph (210 km/hr) at sea level. *Operational ceiling:* 17,060 ft (5,200 m). *Endurance:* 5 hr 0 min. *Armament:* One 7·7 mm machine-gun above upper front fuselage, and one or two 7·7 mm guns in rear cockpit; up to 441 lb (200 kg) of bombs beneath lower wings.

7

Mitsubishi B2M1 of the Ohmura Air Corps, JNAF, *ca* 1932–36. *Engine:* One 600 hp Mitsubishi-built Hispano-Suiza 12-cylinder Vee type. *Span:* 49 ft 11¼ in. (15·22 m). *Length:* 33 ft 8¼ in. (10·27 m). *Height:* 12 ft 2¼ in. (3·712 m). *Take-off weight:* 7,937 lb (3,600 kg). *Maximum speed:* 132 mph (213 km/hr) at sea level. *Operational ceiling:* approx 14,765 ft (4,500 m). *Range:* 597 miles (960 km). *Armament:* One 7·7 mm machine-gun on port side of front fuselage and one in rear cockpit; one 1,764 lb (800 kg) torpedo beneath fuselage or equivalent weight of bombs.

FOX (Belgium)

8
Avions Fairey Fox VIR of the Belgian *Aviation Militaire, ca* 1935. *Engine:* One 860 hp Hispano-Suiza 12 Ydrs 12-cylinder Vee type. *Span:* 37 ft 10¾ in. (11·55 m). *Length:* 30 ft 9 in. (9·37 m). *Height:* 11 ft 6¼ in. (3·51 m). *Take-off weight:* 5,170 lb (2,345 kg). *Maximum speed:* 224 mph (360 km/hr) at 13,123 ft (4,000 m). *Operational ceiling:* 32,808 ft (10,000 m). *Armament:* One 7·62 mm FN-Browning machine-gun each side of front fuselage and one in rear cockpit.

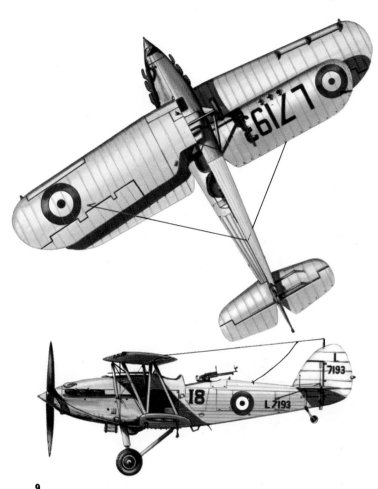

9

Hawker Hind of No 18 Squadron RAF, Upper Heyford (UK), 1937. *Engine:*
One 640 hp Rolls-Royce Kestrel V 12-cylinder Vee type. *Span:* 37 ft 3 in.
(11·35 m). *Length:* 29 ft 3 in. (8·92 m). *Height:* 10 ft 7 in. (3·23 m). *Take-off
weight:* 5,298 lb (2,403 kg). *Maximum speed:* 187 mph (301 km/hr) at 13,120
ft (3,999 m). *Operational ceiling:* 26,400 ft (8,047 m). *Endurance:* 2 hr 55 min.
Armament: One 0·303 in. Vickers machine-gun in port side of front fuselage
and one 0·303 in. Lewis gun in rear cockpit; up to 510 lb (231 kg) of bombs
beneath lower wings.

GORDON (U.K.)

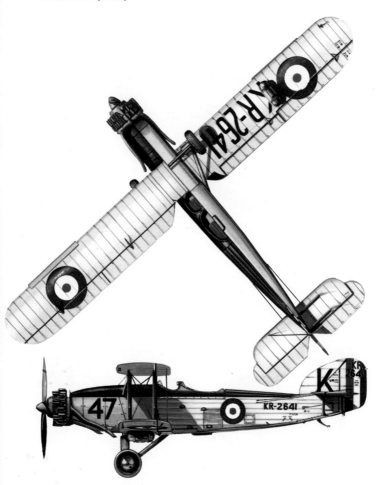

10

Rebuilt Fairey Gordon of No 47 Squadron RAF, Khartoum *ca* 1933–34. *Engine:* One 525 hp Armstrong Siddeley Panther IIA 14-cylinder radial. *Span:* 45 ft 3¼ in. (13·80 m). *Length:* 34 ft 5 in. (10·49 m). *Height:* 12 ft 9 in. (3·89 m). *Take-off weight:* 5,916 lb (2,683 kg). *Maximum speed:* 135 mph (217 km/hr) at sea level. *Operational ceiling:* 16,600 ft (5,060 m). *Range:* 520 miles (837 km). *Armament:* One 0·303 in. Vickers machine-gun on port side of front fuselage and (normally) one 0·303 in. Lewis machine-gun in rear cockpit; provision for up to 460 lb (209 kg) of small bombs beneath lower wings.

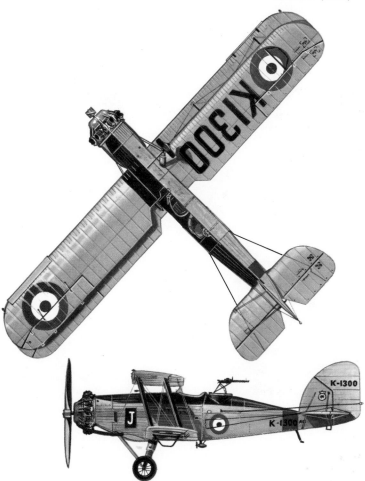

11

Westland Wapiti IIA of No 27 Squadron RAF, Mianwali (India), *ca* 1934.
Engine: One 480 hp Bristol Jupiter VIIIF 9-cylinder radial. *Span:* 46 ft 5 in.
(14·15 m). *Length:* 32 ft 6 in. (9·91 m). *Height:* 11 ft 10 in. (3·61 m). *Take-off
weight:* 5,400 lb (2,449 kg). *Maximum speed:* 140 mph (225 km/hr) at 5,000 ft
(1,524 m). *Operational ceiling:* 20,600 ft (6,279 m). *Range:* 530 miles (853
km). *Armament:* One 0·303 in. Vickers machine-gun on port side of forward
fuselage and one 0·303 in. Lewis gun in rear cockpit; up to 500 lb (227 kg)
of bombs beneath lower wings.

POLIKARPOV U-2 (U.S.S.R.)

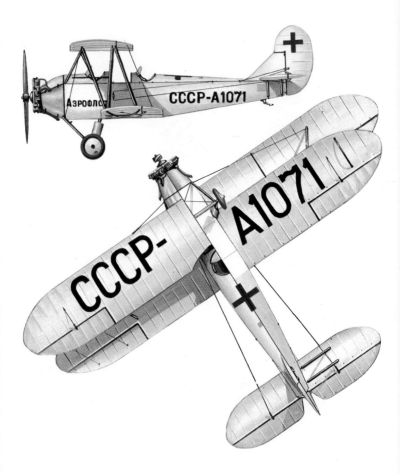

12

Polikarpov U-2SP (Po-2) employed by Aeroflot for ambulance duties, *ca* 1928–29. *Engine:* One 100 hp M-11 5-cylinder radial. *Span:* 37 ft 4¾ in. (11·40 m). *Length:* 26 ft 9¾ in. (8·17 m). *Height:* 9 ft 6¼ in. (2·90 m). *Take-off weight:* 2,205 lb (1,000 kg). *Maximum speed:* 92 mph (148 km/hr) at 6,562 ft (2,000 m). *Operational ceiling:* 10,827 ft (3,300 m). *Range:* 342 miles (550 km). *Armament:* None.

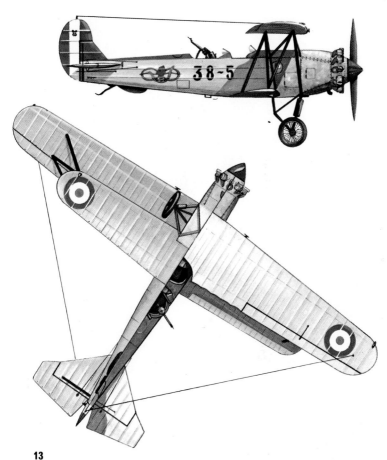

13

IMAM (Meridionali)-built Ro 1 (licence version of Fokker C.V-E), of the 38° *Squadriglia OA, 'Regia Aeronautica,* Ethiopia spring 1936. *Engine:* One 500 hp Alfa Romeo-built Bristol Jupiter 9-cylinder radial. *Span:* 50 ft $2\frac{1}{4}$ in. (15·30 m). *Length:* 31 ft $0\frac{1}{2}$ in. (9·46 m). *Height:* 11 ft 1 in. (3·38 m). *Take-off weight:* 4,795 lb (2,175 kg). *Maximum speed:* 158 mph (255 km/hr) at 9,843 ft (3,000 m). *Operational ceiling:* 19,685 ft (6,000 m). *Maximum range:* 746 miles (1,200 km). *Armament:* One 0·303 in. Vickers machine-gun in upper front fuselage and one 0·303 in Lewis machine-gun in rear cockpit; provision for light bomb load beneath lower wings.

CORSAIR (U.S.A.)

14

Vought SU-1 Special Corsair, staff officer's aircraft of the US Navy, *ca* 1934.
Engine: One 600 hp Pratt & Whitney R-1690-42 Hornet 9-cylinder radial.
Span: 36 ft 0 in. (10·97 m). *Length:* 26 ft 2¼ in. (7·98 m). *Height:* 10 ft 7¾ in.
(3·24 m). *Take-off weight:* 4,765 lb (2,161 kg). *Maximum speed:* 170 mph
(274 km/hr) at 3,000 ft (914 m). *Operational ceiling:* 20,500 ft (6,248 m).
Range: 680 miles (1,094 km). *Armament* (standard SU-1): One 0·30 in.
machine-gun in upper front fuselage and two in rear cockpit.

LETOV S.328 (Czechoslovakia)

15

Letov S.328 (possibly an aircraft of the 2nd Air Regiment) of the Czechoslovak Air Force, *ca* 1934. *Engine:* One 635 hp Walter-built Bristol Pegasus
IIM.2 9-cylinder radial. *Span:* 44 ft. $11\frac{1}{4}$ in. (13·70 m). *Length:* 34 ft $1\frac{1}{2}$ in.
(10·40 m). *Height:* 11 ft 2 in. (3·40 m). *Take-off weight:* 5,820 lb (2,675 kg).
Maximum speed: 174 mph (280 km/hr) at 5,905 ft (1,800 m). *Operational
ceiling:* 23,622 ft (7,200 m). *Normal range:* 435 miles (700 km). *Armament:*
One 7·92 mm Mk 30 machine-gun in each upper wing and two in rear cock
pit; up to 1,102 lb (500 kg) of small bombs beneath fuselage and lower wings.

SWORDFISH (U.K.)

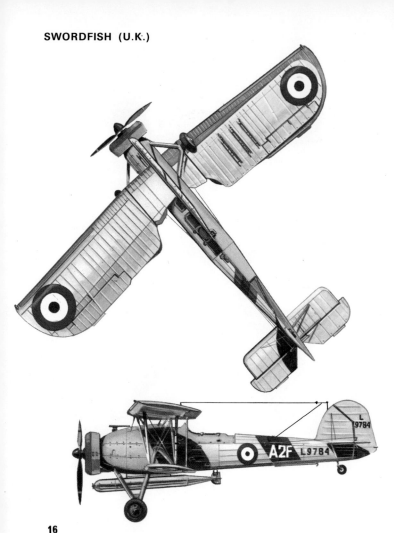

16

Fairey Swordfish I of No 814 Squadron FAA, HMS *Ark Royal*, late 1938.
Engine: One 690 hp Bristol Pegasus IIIM.3 9-cylinder radial. *Span:* 45 ft 6 in.
(13·87 m). *Length:* 36 ft 4 in. (11·07 m). *Height:* 12 ft 10 in. (3·91 m). *Take-off
weight:* 7,720 lb (3,502 kg). *Maximum speed:* 154 mph (248 km/hr) at 7,000 ft
(2,134 m). *Operational ceiling:* 19,250 ft (5,867 m). *Normal range with
torpedo:* 546 miles (879 km). *Armament:* One 0·303 in. Vickers machine-gun
in upper front fuselage and one 0·303 in. Lewis or Vickers K machine-gun in
rear cockpit; one 18 in. torpedo or 1,500 lb (680 kg) mine beneath fuselage,
or equivalent weight of bombs beneath fuselage and lower wings.

17

Vickers Vildebeest IV, aircraft of the officer commanding No 42 Squadron RAF, Donibristle (UK), 1938–39. *Engine:* One 825 hp Bristol Perseus VIII 9-cylinder radial. *Span:* 49 ft 0 in. (14·935 m). *Length:* 37 ft 8 in. (11·48 m). *Height:* 14 ft 8 in. (4·47 m). *Take-off weight:* 8,500 lb (3,855 kg). *Maximum speed:* 156 mph (251 km/hr) at 5,000 ft (1,524 m). *Absolute ceiling:* 19,000 ft (5,791 m). *Maximum range:* 1,625 miles (2,615 km). *Armament:* One 0·303 in. Vickers machine-gun on port side of upper front fuselage and one 0·303 in. Lewis machine-gun in rear cockpit; one 18 in. torpedo or 1,100 lb (499 kg) of bombs beneath fuselage.

CURTISS O2C HELLDIVER (U.S.A.)

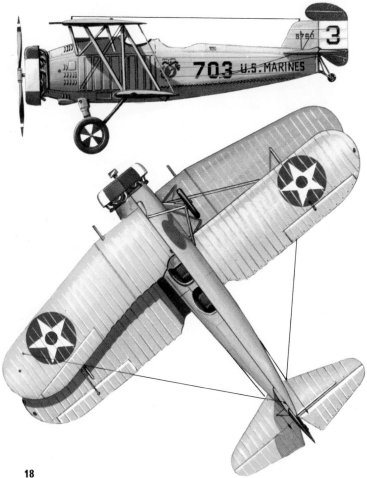

18

Curtiss O2C-1 Helldiver of the US Marine Corps, *ca* 1934. *Engine:* One 450 hp Pratt & Whitney R-1340-4 Wasp 9-cylinder radial. *Span:* 32 ft 0 in. (9·75 m). *Length:* 25 ft 7¾ in. (7·82 m). *Height:* 10 ft 3 in. (3·12 m). *Take-off weight:* 4,020 lb (1,823 kg). *Maximum speed:* 146 mph (235 km/hr) at sea level. *Operational ceiling:* 16,250 ft (4,953 m). *Range:* 720 miles (1,159 km). *Armament:* Two 0·30 in. machine-guns in front fuselage and (normally) one in rear cockpit; provision for one 500 lb (227 kg) or two 116 lb (53 kg) bombs beneath fuselage.

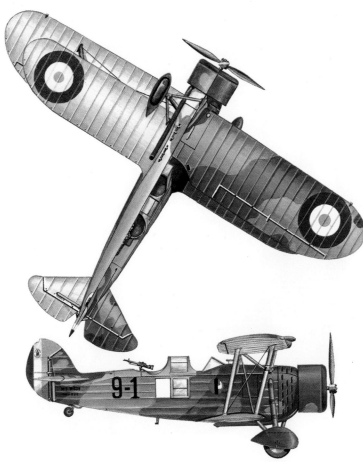

19

IMAM (Meridionali) Ro 37*bis* of the 9° *Squadriglia da Osservazione Aerea* of the *Regia Aeronautica*, Ethiopia *ca* 1937–38. *Engine:* One 560 hp Piaggio P.IX RC 40 9-cylinder radial. *Span:* 36 ft 4¼ in. (11·08 m). *Length:* 28 ft 1 in. (8·56 m). *Height:* 10 ft 4 in. (3·15 m). *Take-off weight:* 5,346 lb (2,425 kg). *Maximum speed:* 199 mph (320 km/hr) at 16,404 ft (5,000 m). *Operational ceiling:* 23,622 ft (7,200 m). *Maximum range:* 932 miles (1,500 km). *Armament:* Two 7·7 mm Breda-SAFAT machine-guns in upper front fuselage and one in rear cockpit; provision for twelve 26 or 33 lb (12 or 15 kg) bombs beneath the fuselage.

CURTISS SBC HELLDIVER (U.S.A.)

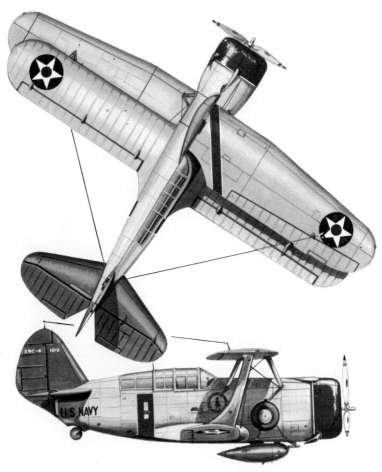

20

Curtiss SBC-4 Helldiver of the US Navy, USS *Enterprise ca* autumn 1939.
Engine: One 950 hp Wright R-1820-34 Cyclone 9-cylinder radial. *Span:*
34 ft 0 in. (10·36 m). *Length:* 27 ft 6¾ in. (8·40 m). *Height:* 13 ft 2 in. (4·01
m). *Take-off weight:* 7,141 lb (3,239 kg). *Maximum speed:* 237 mph (381
km/hr) at 15,200 ft (4,633 m). *Operational ceiling:* 27,300 ft (9,144 m).
Range: 555 miles (893 km). *Armament:* One 0·30 in. machine-gun in upper
front fuselage (stbd) and one in rear cockpit; one 500 lb (227 kg) or 1,000 lb
(454 kg) bomb beneath fuselage.

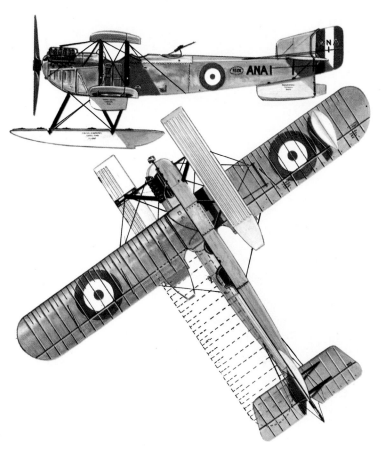

21

Fairey IIIC, first aircraft for the Australian Naval Air Service, as launched at Hamble on 12 August 1921. *Engine:* One 375 hp Rolls-Royce Eagle VIII 12-cylinder Vee type. *Span:* 46 ft 1¼ in. (14·05 m). *Length:* 36 ft 0 in. (10·97 m). *Height:* 12 ft 1¾ in. (3·70 m). *Take-off weight:* 4,800 lb (2,177 kg). *Maximum speed:* 110·5 mph (179 km/hr) at 2,000 ft (610 m). *Operational ceiling:* 15,000 ft (4,572 m). *Endurance:* 5 hr 30 min. *Armament:* One 0·303 in. Vickers machine-gun in front fuselage and one 0·303 in Lewis gun in rear cockpit; provision for small bombs beneath lower wings.

MARTIN T3M (U.S.A.)

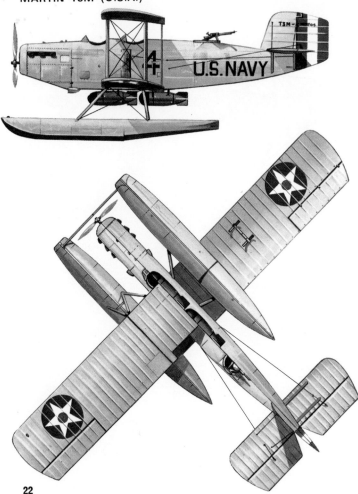

22

Martin T3M-2 of the US Navy, *ca* 1927–28. *Engine:* One 770 hp Packard 3A-2500 6-cylinder in-line. *Span:* 56 ft 7 in. (17·25 m). *Length:* 41 ft 4 in. (12·60 m). *Height:* 15 ft 1 in. (4·60 m). *Take-off weight:* 9,503 lb (4,310 kg). *Maximum speed:* 109 mph (175 km/hr) at sea level. *Operational ceiling:* 7,900 ft (2,408 m). *Range with torpedo:* 634 miles (1,020 km). *Armament:* One 0·30 in. machine-gun in rear cockpit; one 18 in. torpedo or equivalent load of small bombs beneath fuselage.

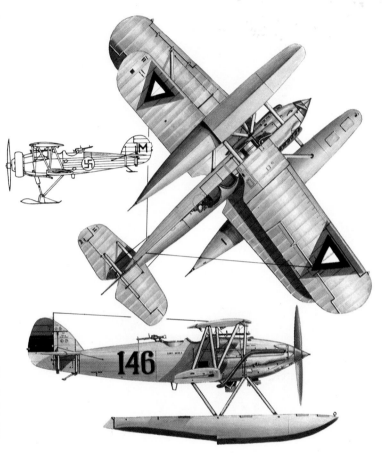

23

Hawker Hart floatplane in Estonian Air Force insignia, *ca* late 1932. *Engine:* One 525 hp Rolls-Royce Kestrel IIS 12-cylinder Vee type. *Span:* 37 ft 3 in. (11·35 m). *Length:* approx 32 ft 7 in. (9·93 m). *Height:* approx 13 ft 6 in. (4·11 m). *Take-off weight:* 4,554 lb (2,066 kg). *Maximum speed:* 184 mph (296 km/hr) at 5,000 ft (1,524 m). *Operational ceiling:* 21,350 ft (6,507 m). 470 miles (756 km). *Armament:* One 0·303 in. Vickers machine-gun on port side of forward fuselage and one 0·303 in. Lewis gun in rear cockpit; up to 520 lb (236 kg) of small bombs beneath lower wings. (Weight and performance data are for landplane; inset view shows version in service with Swedish Air Force, with 580 hp Pegasus IM.2 radial engine.)

DOUGLAS DT-2 (U.S.A.)

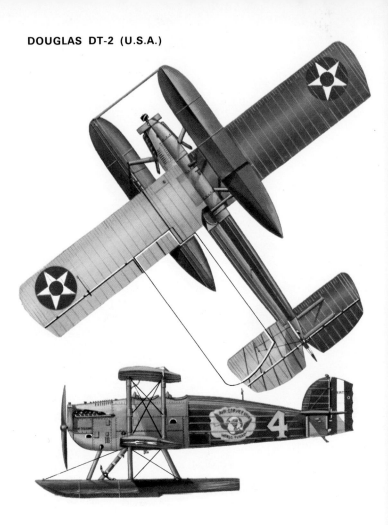

24
Douglas DWC World Cruiser (modified DT-2) of the US Army Air Service,
flown by Lts Nelson and Harding, spring/summer 1924. *Data are for seaplane
version. Engine:* One 420 hp V-1650 Liberty 12A 12-cylinder Vee type. *Span:*
50 ft 0 in. (15·24 m). *Length:* 37 ft 8 in. (11·48 m). *Height:* 15 ft 1 in. (4·60
m). *Take-off weight:* 7,715 lb (3,499 kg). *Maximum speed:* 100 mph (161
km/hr) at sea level. *Operational ceiling:* 7,000 ft (2,134 m). *Range:* 1,650
miles (2,655 km). *Armament:* None.

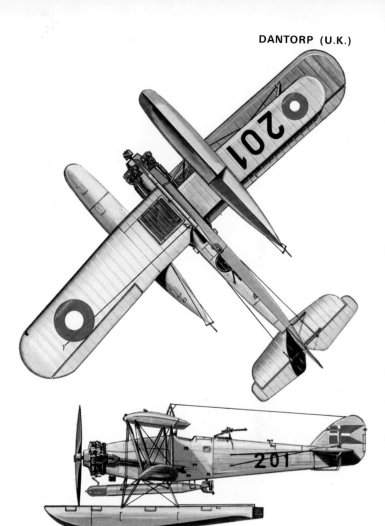

25

Hawker H.B. III (Hydro-Biplane Type III) Dantorp of the 1st *Luftflotille*,
Danish Naval Flying Service, 1933. *Engine:* One 805 hp Armstrong Siddeley
Leopard IIIA 14-cylinder radial. *Span:* 56 ft 5¾ in. (17·21 m). *Length:* 45 ft
11½ in. (14,00 m). *Height:* 18 ft 1 in. (5·51 m). *Take-off weight:* 10,440 lb
(4,736 kg). *Maximum speed:* 128 mph (206 km/hr) at 9,843 ft (3,000 m).
Operational ceiling: 12,500 ft (3,810 m). *Range:* 840 miles (1,352 km).
Armament: One 8 mm Madsen M.32/b machine-gun in forward fuselage and
one 8 mm M.27/a gun in rear cockpit; provision for one 1,565 lb (710 kg)
Type F or K torpedo beneath fuselage and/or eight 110 lb (50 kg) bombs
beneath lower wings. 41

SHARK (U.K.)

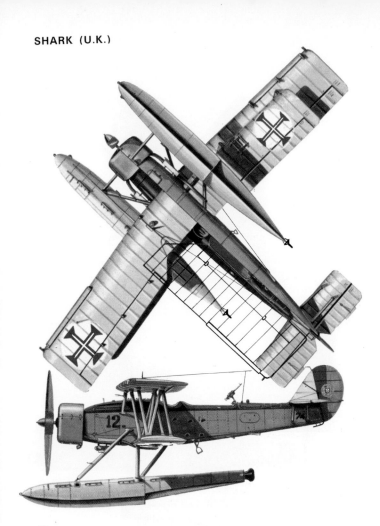

26
Blackburn Shark II supplied to the Portuguese *Direccao da Aeronautica Naval*, 1936. *Engine:* One 700 hp Armstrong Siddeley Tiger VIC 14-cylinder radial. *Span:* 46 ft 0 in. (14·02 m). *Length:* 38 ft 5 in. (11·71 m). *Height:* 15 ft 6 in. (4·72 m). *Take-off weight:* 8,250 lb (3,742 kg). *Maximum speed:* 143 mph (230 km/hr) at 5,500 ft (1,676 m). *Operational ceiling:* 15,250 ft (4,648 m). *Normal range:* 690 miles (1,110 km). *Armament:* One 0·303 in. Vickers machine-gun in port side of upper front fuselage, and one 0·303 in. Vickers-Berthier machine-gun in rear cockpit; one 1,500 lb (680 kg) torpedo beneath fuselage, or equivalent load of bombs.

SEAGULL (U.S.A.)

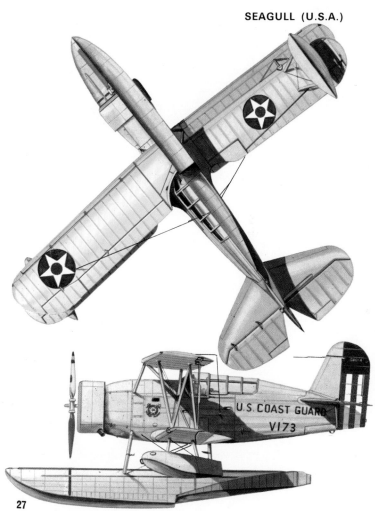

27

Curtiss SOC-4 Seagull of the US Coast Guard, Port Angeles (USA) 1938–39. *Data apply to SOC-1 seaplane. Engine:* One 600 hp Pratt & Whitney R-1340-22 Wasp 9-cylinder radial. *Span:* 36 ft 0 in. (10·97 m). *Length:* 31 ft 7¼ in. (9·63 m). *Height:* 14 ft 8¾ in. (4·49 m). *Take-off weight:* 5,437 lb (2,466 kg). *Maximum speed:* 165 mph (266 km/hr) at 5,000 ft (1,524 m). *Operational ceiling:* 14,900 ft (4,542 m). *Range:* 675 miles (1,086 km). *Armament:* One 0·30 in. Browning machine-gun in lower port wing and one in rear cockpit; provision for one 116 lb (53 kg) bomb beneath each lower wing.

VIMY (U.K.)

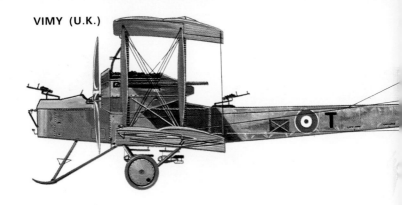

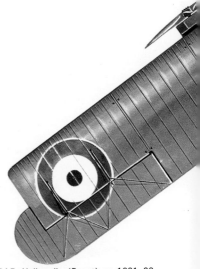

28
Vickers Vimy IV of No 70 Squadron RAF, Heliopolis (Egypt) *ca* 1921–22.
Engines: Two 360 hp Rolls-Royce Eagle VIII 12-cylinder Vee type. *Span:*
68 ft 0 in. (20·73 m). *Length:* 43 ft 6½ in. (13·27 m). *Height:* 15 ft 7½ in. (4·76
m). *Take-off weight:* 12,500 lb (5,670 kg). *Maximum speed:* 103 mph (166
km/hr) at sea level. *Operational ceiling:* 7,000 ft (2,314 m). *Range:* approx
900 miles (1,448 km). *Armament:* One 0·303 in. Lewis machine-gun in nose
and one in rear cockpit; up to 2,476 lb (1,123 kg) of bombs beneath fuselage
and lower wings.

D.H.10 (U.K.)

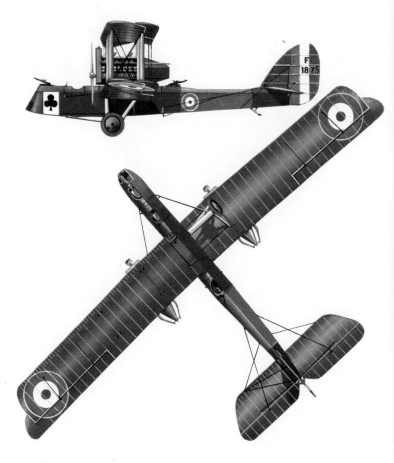

29
De Havilland D.H.10 Amiens of No 216 Squadron, RAF Heliopolis, Egypt, 1922. *Engines:* Two 396 hp V-1650 Liberty 12 12-cylinder Vee type. *Span:* 65 ft 6 in. (19·96 m). *Length:* 39 ft 7½ in. (12·08 m). *Height:* 15 ft 0 in. (4·57 m). *Normal take-off weight:* 9,000 lb (4,082 kg). *Maximum speed:* 126 mph (203 km/hr) at 6,500 ft (1,981 m). *Operational ceiling:* 17,500 ft (5,334 m). *Endurance:* 5 hr 45 min. *Armament:* One 0·303 in. Lewis machine-gun (occasionally two) in each of nose and rear cockpits; up to six 230 lb (370 kg) bombs or equivalent weight in smaller weapons.

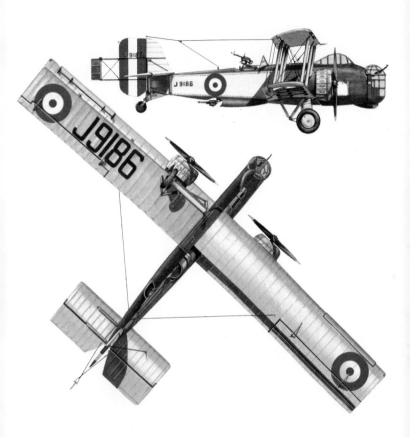

30

Prototype Boulton and Paul Overstrand (converted Sidestrand III), used for trials by manufacturer and by No 101 Squadron RAF, 1933–34. *Data apply to production version. Engines:* Two 580 hp Bristol Pegasus IIM.3 9-cylinder radials. *Span:* 71 ft 11¼ in. (21·93 m). *Length:* 46 ft 1¾ in. (14·065 m). *Height:* 15 ft 9 in. (4·80 m). *Take-off weight:* 12,000 lb (5,443 kg). *Maximum speed:* 153 mph (246 km/hr) at 6,500 ft (1,981 m). *Operational ceiling:* 22,500 ft (6,858 m). *Range:* 545 miles (877 km). *Armament:* Three 0·303 in. Lewis machine-guns, one each in nose turret, rear cockpit and ventral position; up to 1,600 lb (726 kg) of bombs internally.

MARTIN MB-2 (U.S.A.)

31

Curtiss NBS-1 (Martin MB-2) Type XII of the 25th Bombardment Squadron, US Army Air Service, *ca* 1924. *Engines:* Two 420 hp V-1650 Liberty 12A 12-cylinder Vee type. *Span:* 74 ft 2 in. (22·61 m). *Length:* 42 ft 8 in. (13·00 m). *Height:* 14 ft 8 in. (4·47 m). *Normal take-off weight:* 12,064 lb (5,472 kg). *Maximum speed:* 99 mph (159 km/hr) at sea level. Operational ceiling: 8,500 ft (2,591 m). *Range:* 558 miles (898 km). *Armament:* Five 0·30 in. machine-guns, two each in nose and dorsal positions and one in ventral position; up to 2,000 lb (907 kg) of bombs internally and/or externally.

KEYSTONE B-4A (U.S.A.)

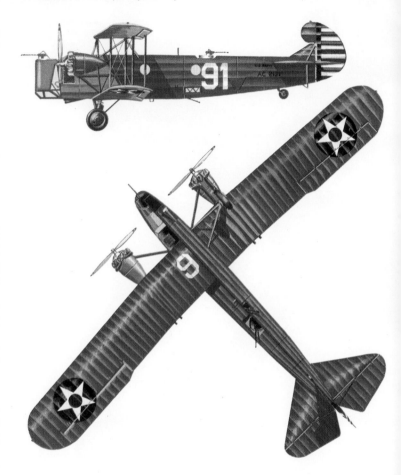

32
Keystone B-4A of the US Army Air Corps, *ca* 1933. *Engines:* Two 575 hp
Pratt & Whitney R-1860-7 Hornet 9-cylinder radials. *Span:* 74 ft 9 in. (22·78
m). *Length:* 48 ft 10 in. (14·88 m). *Height:* 15 ft 9 in. (4·80 m). *Take-off
weight:* 13,209 lb (5,992 kg). *Maximum speed:* 121 mph (195 km/hr) at sea
level. *Operational ceiling:* 14,000 ft (4,267 m). *Range:* 855 miles (1,376 km).
Armament: Three 0·30 in. Browning machine-guns, one each in nose, dorsal
and ventral positions; up to 2,500 lb (1,134 kg) of bombs.

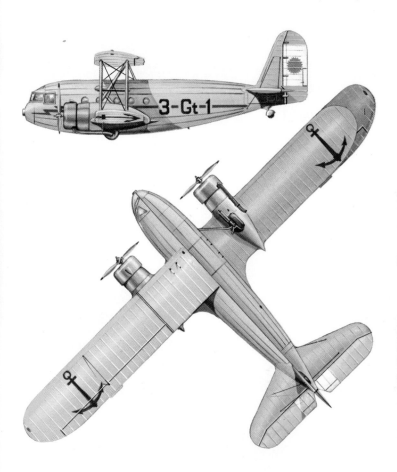

33

Curtiss CT-32 Condor of the 3rd *Grupo de Transporte*, Argentine Navy, Punta del Indio, 1935. *Engines:* Two 760 hp Wright SGR-1820F-52 Cyclone 9-cylinder radials. *Span:* 82 ft 0 in. (24·99 m). *Length:* 48 ft 7 in. (14·81 m). *Height:* 16 ft 4 in. (4·98 m). *Maximum take-off weight:* 18,500 lb (8,392 kg). *Maximum speed:* 184 mph (296 km/hr) at 6,900 ft (2,103 m). *Operational ceiling:* 21,200 ft (7,011 m). *Normal range:* 640 miles (1,030 km). *Armament:* None.

LIORÉ et OLIVIER 20 (France)

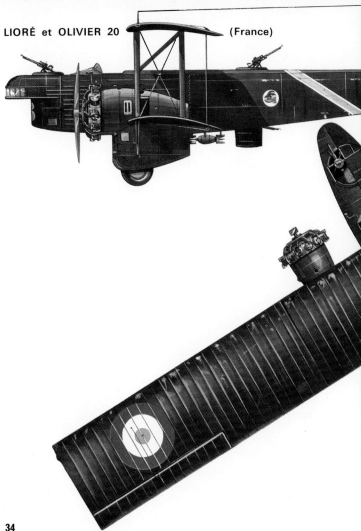

34

Lioré et Olivier LeO 20 Bn.2 of the French *Aviation Militaire, ca* 1929. *Engines:* Two 420 hp Gnome-Rhône 9 Ady (licence Bristol Jupiter) 9-cylinder radials. *Span:* 72 ft 10 in. (22·20 m). *Length:* 45 ft 2 in. (13·77 m). *Height (tail up):* 16 ft 6¾ in. (5·05 m). *Take-off weight:* 12,037 lb (5,460 kg). *Maximum speed:* 123 mph (198 km/hr) at sea level. *Operational ceiling:* 18,865 ft (5,750 m). *Range:* 621 miles (1,000 km). *Armament:* Five 7·7 mm machine-guns, two each in nose and dorsal positions and one in ventral 'dustbin'; up to 1,102 lb (500 kg) of bombs internally and beneath fuselage and lower wings.

VIRGINIA (U.K.)

35

Vickers Virginia X of No 7 Squadron RAF, Bircham Newton (UK) *ca* 1933–34. *Engines:* Two 580 hp Napier Lion VB 12-cylinder 'W' type. *Span:* 87 ft 8 in. (26·72 m). *Length:* 62 ft 3 in. (18·97 m). *Height:* 18 ft 2 in. (5·54 m). *Take-off weight:* 17,600 lb (7,983 kg). *Maximum speed:* 108 mph (174 km/hr) at 5,000 ft (1,524 m). *Operational ceiling:* 15,530 ft (4,734 m). *Range:* 985 miles (1,585 km). *Armament:* One 0·303 in. Lewis machine-gun in nose and two in tail position; up to 3,000 lb (1,361 kg) of bombs.

HINAIDI (U.K.)

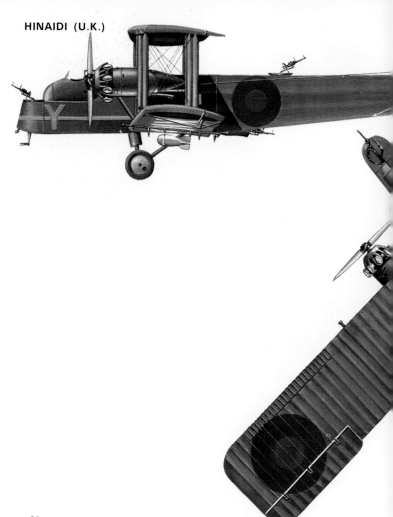

36
Handley Page Hinaidi II of No 99 Squadron RAF, Upper Heyford (UK) *ca* 1930. *Engines:* Two 440 hp Bristol Jupiter VIII 9-cylinder radials. *Span:* 75 ft 0 in. (22·86 m). *Length:* 59 ft 2 in. (18·03 m). *Height:* 17 ft 0 in. (5·18 m). *Take-off weight:* 14,500 lb (6,577 kg). *Maximum speed:* 122·5 mph (197 km/hr) at sea level. *Operational ceiling:* 14,500 ft (4,420 m). *Range:* 800 miles (1,287 km). *Armament:* Three 0·303 in. Lewis machine-guns, one each in nose, dorsal and ventral positions; up to 1,448 lb (657 kg) of bombs beneath fuselage and lower wings.

HEYFORD (U.K.)

37

Handley Page Heyford I of 'A' Flight, No 99 Squadron RAF, Upper Heyford (UK) mid-1934. *Engines:* Two 575 hp Rolls-Royce Kestrel IIIS 12-cylinder Vee type. *Span:* 75 ft 0 in. (22·86 m). *Length:* 58 ft 0 in. (17·68 m). *Height (tail down):* 20 ft 6 in. (6·25 m). *Take-off weight:* 16,750 lb (7,597 kg). *Maximum speed:* 142 mph (229 km/hr) at 12,500 ft (3,810 m). *Operational ceiling:* 21,000 ft (6,401 m). *Range:* 920 miles (1,481 km). *Armament:* Three 0·303 in. Lewis machine-guns, one each in nose and dorsal positions and one in retractable ventral 'dustbin'; up to 3,500 lb (1,588 kg) of bombs in centre-section and below outer panels of lower wing.

KAWASAKI Ki-32 (Japan)

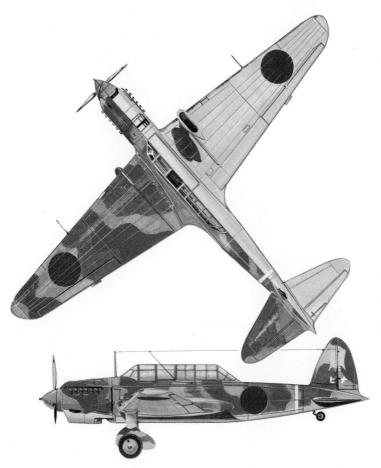

38
Kawasaki Ki-32 of the 3rd Squadron, 45th Group JAAF, *ca* 1938–39. *Engine:*
One 850 hp Kawasaki Ha-9-IIB 12-cylinder Vee type. *Span:* 49 ft 2½ in.
(15·00 m). *Length:* 37 ft 10 in. (11·53 m). *Height:* 9 ft 6¼ in. (2·90 m). *Take-off
weight:* 7,458 lb (3,383 kg). *Maximum speed:* 258 mph (416 km/hr) at
9,843 ft (3,000 m). *Operational ceiling:* 27,887 ft (8,500 m). *Normal range:*
839 miles (1,350 km). *Armament:* One 7·7 mm machine-gun in front fuselage
and two 7·7 mm guns in rear cockpit; up to 661 lb (300 kg) of bombs internally.

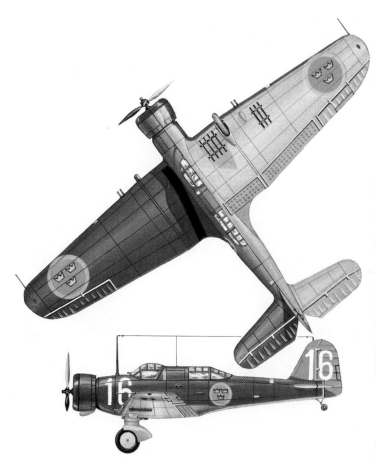

39

Saab-built Northrop 8A-1 (B 5) of F4 Wing Royal Swedish Air Force, 1939.
Engine: One 875 hp Swedish-built Bristol Hercules 14-cylinder radial. *Span:*
47 ft 9 in. (14·55 m). *Length:* 31 ft 9 in. (9·68 m). *Height:* 12 ft 11 in. (3·94 m).
Take-off weight: 7,500 lb (3,402 kg). *Maximum speed:* 219 mph (352 km/hr)
at 6,250 ft (1,905 m). *Operational ceiling:* 22,500 ft (6,858 m). *Maximum
range:* 1,380 miles (2,221 km). *Armament:* Two 0·30 in. Browning machine-
guns in each wing and one in rear cockpit; up to twenty 30 lb (14 kg) bombs
internally or two 120 lb (54 kg) bombs beneath each wing.

DEVASTATOR (U.S.A.)

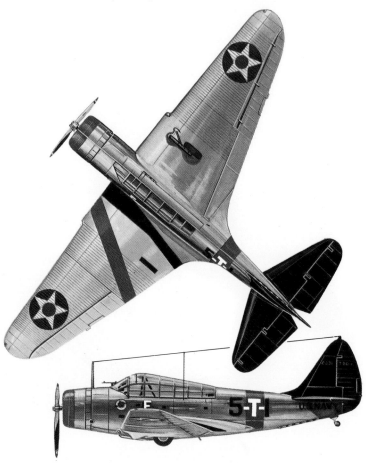

40

Douglas TBD-1 Devastator, commanding officer's aircraft of US Navy Squadron VT-5, USS *Yorktown*, 1939. *Engine:* One 900 hp Pratt & Whitney R-1830-64 Twin Wasp 14-cylinder radial. *Span:* 50 ft 0 in. (15·24 m). *Length:* 35 ft 0 in. (10·67 m). *Height:* 15 ft 1 in. (4·60 m). *Maximum take-off weight:* 10,914 lb (4,951 kg). *Maximum speed:* 206 mph (332 km/hr) at 8,000 ft (2,438 m). *Operational ceiling:* 19,700 ft (6,005 m). *Normal range with torpedo:* 435 miles (700 km). *Armament:* One 0·30 in. machine-gun in upper front fuselage and one 0·50 in. gun in rear cockpit; one 21 in. torpedo or one 1,000 lb (454 kg) bomb internally or externally.

LOIRE-NIEUPORT LN-40 (France)

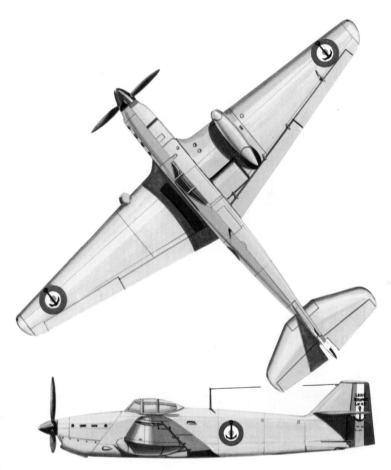

41

Loire-Nieuport LN-42 prototype, as completed in *Aéronavale* insignia and flown in 1945. *Data apply to LN-401. Engine:* One 690 hp Hispano-Suiza 12 Xcrs 12-cylinder Vee type. *Span:* 45 ft 11$\frac{1}{4}$ in. (14·00 m). *Length:* 32 ft. 0$\frac{1}{4}$ in. (9·76 m). *Height:* 11 ft 5$\frac{3}{4}$ in. (3.50 m). *Take-off weight:* 6,250 lb (2,835 kg). *Maximum speed:* 236 mph (380 km/hr) at 13,123 ft (4,000 m). *Operational ceiling:* 31,168 ft (9,500 m). *Range:* 746 miles (1,200 km). *Armament:* One 20 mm Hispano cannon firing through the propeller hub and one 7·5 mm Darne machine-gun in each wing; one bomb of up to 496 lb (225 kg) beneath fuselage.

HEINKEL He 70 (Germany)

42

Heinkel He 70F-1 of the 2nd *Staffel*, *Aufklärungsgruppe* I, *Luftkreiskommando*
II (Berlin), *ca* 1935. *Engine:* One 750 hp BMW VI 7·3 12-cylinder Vee type.
Span: 48 ft 6¾ in. (14·80 m). *Length:* 38 ft 4¾ in. (11·70 m). *Height:* 10 ft 2 in.
(3·10 m). *Take-off weight:* 7,540 lb (3,420 kg). *Maximum speed:* 224 mph
(360 km/hr) at 13,123 ft (4,000 m). *Operational ceiling:* 17,224 ft (5,250 m).
Range: 497 miles (800 km). *Armament:* One 7·9 mm MG 15 machine-gun
in rear cockpit.

43

Vickers Wellesley of the RAF Long Range Development Unit, flown by Sqn Ldr R. Kellett; one of three aircraft taking part in the world distance record attempt 5–7 November 1938. *Data are for standard Wellesley I. Engine:* One 925 hp Bristol Pegasus XX 9-cylinder radial. *Span:* 74 ft 7 in. (22·73 m). *Length:* 39 ft 3 in. (11·96 m). *Height:* 12 ft 4 in. (3·76 m). *Take-off weight:* (*normal*): 11,100 lb (5,035 kg); (*record aircraft*): 18,400 lb (8,346 kg). *Maximum speed:* 264 mph (425 km/hr) at 19,680 ft (5,998 m). *Operational ceiling:* 33,000 ft (10,058 m). *Range:* 2,590 miles (4,168 km). (Record aircraft flew 7,157·7 miles—11,519 km). *Armament:* One 0·303 in. Vickers machine-gun in port wing and one 0·303 in. Vickers K machine-gun in rear cockpit; 2,000 lb (907 kg) of bombs in two underwing containers.

AMIOT 143 (France)

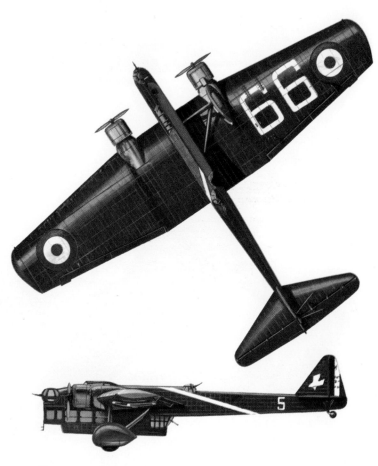

44

Amiot 143M of the 4e *Escadrille*, GB II/22 of the *Armée de l'Air*, Chartres late 1935. *Engines:* Two 760 hp Gnome-Rhône 14 Kirs/Kjrs 14-cylinder radials. *Span:* 80 ft 6½ in. (24·55 m). *Length:* 59 ft 10 in. (18·24 m). *Height:* 18 ft 7½ in. (5·68 m). *Normal take-off weight:* 18,984 lb (8,611 kg). *Maximum speed:* 183 mph (294·5 km/hr) at 11,483 ft (3,500 m). *Operational ceiling:* 25,919 ft (7,900 m). *Range:* 746 miles (1,200 km). *Armament:* Four 7·5 mm MAC 1934 machine-guns, one each in nose and dorsal turrets and fore and aft in ventral gondola; up to 1,984 lb (900 kg) of bombs internally, plus four bombs of up to 441 lb (200 kg) each beneath the wings.

45

Bloch 200 Bn4 of the 1e *Escadrille*, GB I/12 of the *Armée de l'Air*, Reims 1937. *Engines:* Two 870 hp Gnome-Rhône 14 Kirs/Kjrs 14-cylinder radials. *Span:* 73 ft 7¾ in. (22·45 m). *Length:* 52 ft 6 in. (16·00 m). *Height:* 12 ft 10¼ in. (3·92 m). *Normal take-off weight:* 16,050 lb (7,280 kg). *Maximum speed:* 143 mph (230 km/hr) at 14,108 ft (4,300 m). *Operational ceiling:* 22,638 ft (6,900 m). *Range:* 621 miles (1,000 km). *Armament:* Three 7·5 mm MAC 1934 machine-guns, one each in nose, dorsal and ventral turrets; normal internal bomb load of 3,307 lb (1,500 kg).

POTEZ 540 (France)

46

Potez 540 (possibly an aircraft of GC II/1) of the *Armée de l'Air, ca* 1936. *Engines:* Two 690 hp Hispano-Suiza 12 Xirs/Xjrs 12-cylinder Vee type. *Span:* 72 ft 6 in. (22·10 m). *Length:* 53 ft 1¾ in. (16·20 m). *Height:* 12 ft 8¾ in. (3·88 m). *Take-off weight:* 13,117 lb (5,950 kg). *Maximum speed:* 193 mph (310 km/hr) at 13,123 ft (4,000 m). *Operational ceiling:* 32,808 ft (10,000 m). *Normal range:* 746 miles (1,200 km). *Armament:* Three to five 7·7 mm machine-guns, one in nose turret and one or two each in dorsal turret and ventral enclosure; up to 2,205 lb (1,000 kg) of bombs.

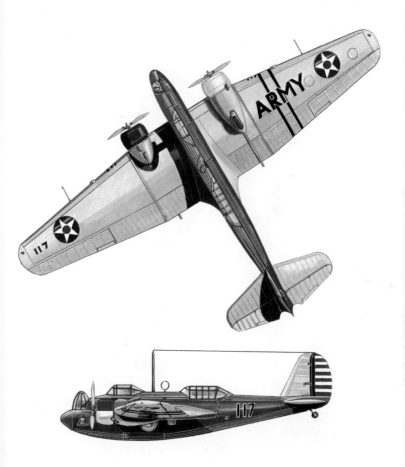

47
Martin B-10B of the 31st Bombardment Squadron, 3rd Bombing Group of the USAAC, *ca* 1935. *Engines:* Two 775 hp Wright R-1820-33 Cyclone 9-cylinder radials. *Span:* 70 ft 6 in. (21·49 m). *Length:* 44 ft 8¾ in. (13·63 m). *Height (tail down):* 11 ft 5 in. (3·48 m). *Normal take-off weight:* 14,600 lb (6,622 kg). *Maximum speed:* 213 mph (343 km/hr) at 10,000 ft (3,048 m). *Operational ceiling:* 24,200 ft (7,376 m). *Normal range:* 590 miles (950 km). *Armament:* Three 0·30 in. Browning machine-guns, one each in nose turret and dorsal and ventral positions; up to 2,200 lb (998 kg) of bombs internally or 2,000 lb (907 kg) externally.

HEINKEL He 111 (Germany)

48

Heinkel He 111B-1 prior to delivery to KG 154 of the *Luftwaffe*, autumn 1936. *Engines:* Two 1,000 hp Daimler-Benz DB 600Aa 12-cylinder inverted-Vee type. *Span:* 74 ft 1¾ in. (22·60 m). *Length:* 57 ft 5 in. (17·50 m). *Height:* 14 ft 5¼ in. (4·40 m). *Maximum take-off weight:* 20,536 lb (9,315 kg). *Maximum speed:* 248 mph (400 km/hr) at 13,123 ft (4,000 m). *Operational ceiling:* 22,966 ft (7,000 m). *Range:* 559 miles (900 km). *Armament:* Three 7·9 mm MG 15 machine-guns, one each in nose and dorsal positions and one in retractable ventral 'dustbin'; up to 3,307 lb (1,500 kg) of bombs internally.

49

Bristol Blenheim I of No 44 Squadron RAF, Waddington (UK) May 1938.
Engines: Two 730 hp Bristol Mercury VIII 9-cylinder radials. *Span:* 56 ft 4 in.
(17·17 m). *Length:* 39 ft 9 in. (12·12 m). *Height (tail down):* 9 ft 10 in. (3·00
m). *Take-off weight:* 12,500 lb (5,670 kg). *Maximum speed:* 285 mph (459
km/hr) at 15,000 ft (4,572 m). *Operational ceiling:* 27,280 ft (8,315 m).
Range: 1,125 miles (1,810 km). *Armament:* One 0·303 in. Browning machine-
gun in port wing and one 0·303 in. Vickers K machine-gun in dorsal turret;
up to 1,000 lb (454 kg) of bombs internally.

TUPOLEV SB-2 (U.S.S.R.)

50
Tupolev SB-2 (ANT-40) of the Chinese Air Force, *ca* 1937. *Engines:* Two
830 hp M-100 12-cylinder Vee type. *Span:* 66 ft 8½ in. (20·33 m). *Length:*
40 ft 3¼ in. (12·27 m). *Height:* 10 ft 8 in. (3·25 m). *Take-off weight:* 13,448 lb
(6,100 kg). *Maximum speed:* 255 mph (410 km/hr) at 13,123 ft (4,000 m).
Operational ceiling: 27,887 ft (8,500 m). *Range:* 746 miles (1,200 km).
Armament: Four 7·62 mm ShKAS machine-guns, two in nose and one each
in dorsal and ventral positions; up to 2,205 lb (1,000 kg) of bombs internally.

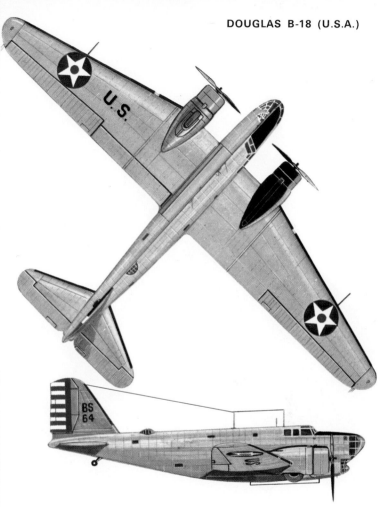

51

Douglas B-18A of the USAAC, *ca* 1939. *Engines:* Two 1,000 hp Wright R-1820-53 Cyclone 9-cylinder radials. *Span:* 89 ft 6 in. (27·28 m). *Length:* 57 ft 10 in. (17·63 m). *Height:* 15 ft 2 in. (4·62 m). *Take-off weight:* 27,673 lb (12,552 kg). *Maximum speed:* 215 mph (346 km/hr) at 10,000 ft (3,048 m). *Operational ceiling:* 23,900 ft (7,285 m). *Range:* 1,200 miles (1,931 km). *Armament:* One 0·30 in. machine-gun in each of nose, dorsal and ventral positions; up to 6,500 lb (2,948 kg) of bombs internally.

DORNIER Do 23 (Germany)

52
Dornier Do 23G of the 5th *Staffel*, II *Gruppe*, 2nd *Geschwader*, *Luftkreis-kommando* III (Dresden) 1936. *Engines:* Two 750 hp BMW VI U 12-cylinder Vee type. *Span:* 83 ft 11¾ in. (25·60 m). *Length:* 61 ft 7¼ in. (18·775 m). *Height:* 17 ft 8½ in. (5·40 m). *Normal take-off weight:* 19,290 lb (8,750 kg). *Maximum speed:* 162 mph (260 km/hr) at 984 ft (300 m). *Operational ceiling:* 19,029 ft (5,800 m). *Normal range:* 746 miles (1,200 km). *Armament:* One 7·9 mm MG 15 machine-gun in each of nose, dorsal and ventral positions; up to 2,205 lb (1,000 kg) of bombs internally.

CAPRONI Ca 310 (Italy)

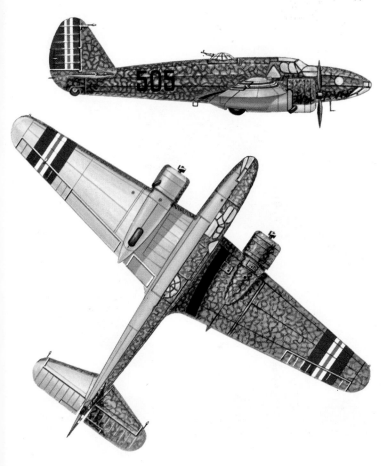

53
Caproni Ca 310 of the Norwegian Air Force, *ca* 1939. *Engines:* Two 470 hp
Piaggio P.VII C 35 7-cylinder radials. *Span:* 53 ft 1¾ in. (16·20 m). *Length:*
40 ft 0¼ in. (12·20 m). *Height:* 11 ft 7 in. (3·52 m). *Take-off weight:* 10,252 lb
(4,650 kg). *Maximum speed:* 227 mph (365 km/hr) at 9,843 ft (3,000 m).
Operational ceiling: 22,966 ft (7,000 m). *Range:* 1,025 miles (1,650 km).
Armament: One 7·7 mm machine-gun in each wing and one in dorsal turret;
up to 882 lb (400 kg) of bombs internally.

HARROW (U.K.)

54

Handley Page Harrow I of No 214 Squadron RAF, Feltwell (UK) mid-1937. (N.B.—fuselage codes should read 214-K.) *Engines:* Two 830 hp Bristol Pegasus X 9-cylinder radials. *Span:* 88 ft 5 in. (26·95 m). *Length:* 82 ft 2 in. (25·04 m). *Height:* 19 ft 5 in. (5·85 m). *Take-off weight:* 23,000 lb (10,433 kg). *Maximum speed:* 190 mph (306 km/hr) at 10,000 ft (3,048 m). *Operational ceiling:* 19,200 ft (5,852 m). *Normal range:* 1,250 miles (2,253 km). *Armament:* Four 0·303 in. Browning machine-guns, one each in nose and dorsal turrets and two in tail turret; up to 3,000 lb (1,361 kg) of bombs internally.

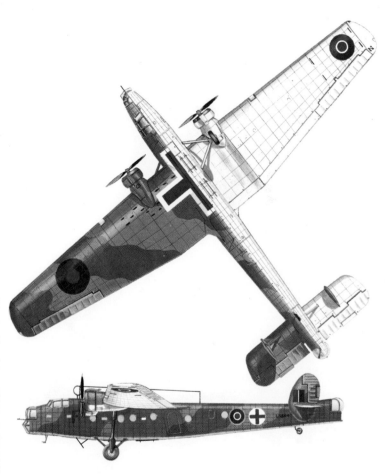

55
Short-built Bristol Bombay of No 1 Air Ambulance Unit RAAF, Tunis May 1943. *Engines:* Two 1,010 hp Bristol Pegasus XXII 9-cylinder radials. *Span:* 95 ft 9 in. (29·18 m). *Length:* 69 ft 3 in. (21·11 m). *Height (tail down):* 19 ft 6 in. (5·94 m). *Take-off weight:* 20,000 lb (9,072 kg). *Maximum speed:* 192 mph (309 km/hr) at 6,500 ft (1,981 m). *Operational ceiling:* 25,000 ft (7,620 m). *Normal range:* 880 miles (1,416 km). *Armament* (as bomber—deleted from ambulance version): One 0·303 in. Vickers K machine-gun in each of nose and tail turrets; up to 2,000 lb (907 kg) of bombs internally.

MITSUBISHI Ki-2 (Japan)

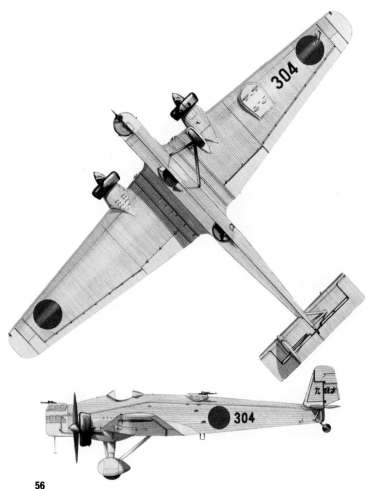

56

Mitsubishi Ki-2-I (fourth prototype) of the Army 7th Air Wing, JAAF, *ca* 1933–34. *Engines:* Two 570 hp Nakajima Kotobuki 9-cylinder radials. *Span:* 65 ft 6 in. (19·962 m). *Length:* 41 ft 4 in. (12·60 m). *Height:* 15 ft 2½ in. (4·635 m). *Take-off weight:* 10,031 lb (4,550 kg). *Maximum speed:* 158 mph (255 km/hr) at 9,843 ft (3,000 m). *Operational ceiling:* 22,966 ft (7,000 m). *Range:* 559 miles (900 km). *Armament:* One 7·7 mm machine-gun in nose and one in dorsal position; up to 661 lb (300 kg) of bombs internally.

MITSUBISHI G3M (Japan)

57

Mitsubishi G3M3 Model 23 of the Genzan Naval Air Corps, JNAF, 1941. *Engines:* Two 1,300 hp Mitsubishi Kinsei 53 14-cylinder radials. *Span:* 82 ft 0¼ in. (25·00 m). *Length:* 53 ft 11¾ in. (16·45 m). *Height:* 14 ft 11½ in. (4·56 m). *Take-off weight:* 17,857 lb (8,100 kg). *Maximum speed:* 258 mph (416 km/hr) at 19,357 ft (5,900 m). *Operational ceiling:* 33,727 ft (10,280 m). *Maximum range:* 2,090 miles (3,363 km). *Armament:* One 20 mm cannon in dorsal turret and two 7·7 mm machine-guns in each waist blister; up to 1,764 lb (800 kg) of bombs internally.

DORNIER Do 17 (Germany)

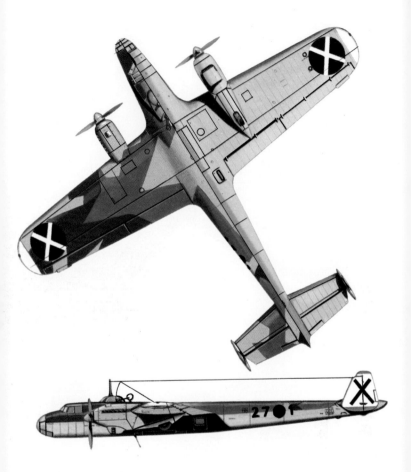

58

Dornier Do 17F-1 of *Aufklärungsstaffel* 1.A/88, Condor Legion, Spain October 1937. *Engines:* Two 750 hp BMW VI 7·3 12-cylinder Vee type. *Span:* 59 ft 0¾ in. (18·00 m). *Length:* 53 ft 3¾ in. (16·25 m). *Height:* 14 ft 2 in. (4·32 m). *Take-off weight:* 15,432 lb (7,000 kg). *Maximum speed:* 222 mph (357 km/hr) at sea level. *Operational ceiling:* 19,685 ft (6,000 m). *Maximum range:* 1,274 miles (2,050 km). *Armament:* One 7·9 mm MG 15 machine-gun at rear of crew cabin and one in lower front fuselage; up to 1,653 lb (750 kg) of bombs internally.

JUNKERS Ju 86 (Germany)

59

Junkers Ju 86K-4 (B 3A) of F1 Wing Royal Swedish Air Force, Västeras *ca* autumn 1938. *Engines:* Two 820 hp Swedish-built Bristol Mercury III 9-cylinder radials. *Span:* 73 ft 9 in. (22·48 m). *Length:* 58 ft 8 in. (17·88 m). *Height:* 15 ft 8¼ in. (4·78 m). *Take-off weight:* 18,078 lb (8,200 kg). *Maximum speed:* 224 mph (360 km/hr) at 13,123 ft (4,000 m). *Operational ceiling:* 22,966 ft (7,000 m). *Maximum range:* 1,243 miles (2,000 km). *Armament:* Three 7·9 mm MG 15 machine-guns, one each in nose and dorsal positions and one in ventral 'dustbin'; up to 2,205 lb (1,000 kg) of bombs internally.

BREGUET 691 (France)

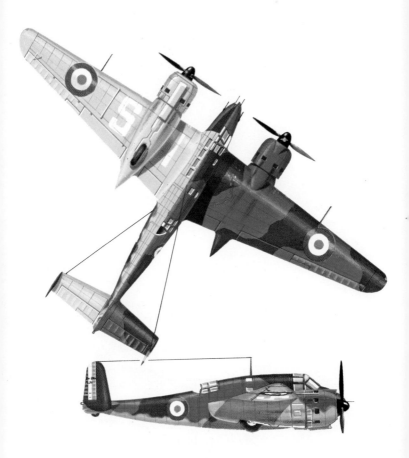

60

Breguet 691 AB.2, ex works aircraft prior to delivery to the *Armée de l'Air,
ca* spring 1939. *Engines:* Two 700 hp Hispano-Suiza 14AB-10/11 14-
cylinder radials. *Span:* 50 ft 4¾ in. (15·36 m). *Length:* 32 ft 1¾ in. (9·80 m).
Height: 13 ft 1½ in. (4·00 m). *Maximum take-off weight:* 11,023 lb (5,000
kg). *Maximum speed:* 301 mph (485 km/hr) at 13,123 ft (4,000 m). *Operational ceiling:* 27,887 ft (8,500 m). *Maximum range:* 808 miles (1,300 km).
Armament: One 20 mm Hispano cannon and two 7·5 mm MAC 1934 machine-
guns in nose, and one MAC 1934 gun in each of dorsal and ventral positions;
up to 882 lb (400 kg) of bombs internally.

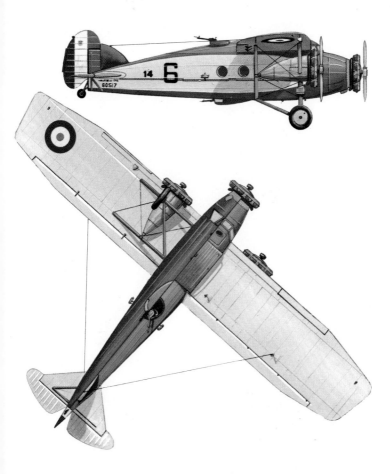

61

Caproni Ca 101 D.2 of the *Regia Aeronautica*, Italian East Africa *ca* 1933. *Engines:* Three 240 hp Alfa Romeo D.2 9-cylinder radials. *Span:* 64 ft 6¾ in. (19·68 m). *Length:* 45 ft 3¼ in. (13·80 m). *Height:* 12 ft 9¼ in. (3·89 m). *Take-off weight:* 10,968 lb (4,975 kg). *Maximum speed:* 103 mph (165 km/hr) at 3,281 ft (1,000 m). *Operational ceiling:* 20,013 ft (6,100 m). *Range:* 621 miles (1,000 km). *Armament:* One 7·7 mm machine-gun in dorsal position and one or two in ventral position; provision for up to 1,102 lb (500 kg) of bombs internally and externally.

JUNKERS Ju 52/3m (Germany)

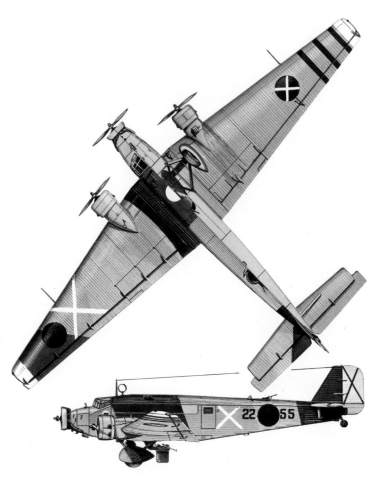

62

Junkers Ju 52/3mg3e of *Grupo* 2-G-22, Spanish Nationalist Air Force, *ca*
1936. *Engines:* Three 600 hp BMW 132A (licence Pratt & Whitney Hornet)
9-cylinder radials. *Span:* 95 ft 11½ in. (29·25 m). *Length:* 62 ft 0 in. (18·90 m).
Height (tail down): 14 ft 9¼ in. (4·50 m). *Take-off weight:* 20,944 lb (9,500 kg).
Maximum speed: 180 mph (290 km/hr) at sea level. *Operational ceiling:*
20,669 ft. (6,300 m). *Range:* 795 miles (1,280 km). *Armament:* Two 7·9 mm
MG 15 machine-guns, one in dorsal position and one in ventral 'dustbin';
up to 2,205 lb (1,000 kg) of bombs internally.

SAVOIA-MARCHETTI S.M.81 (Italy)

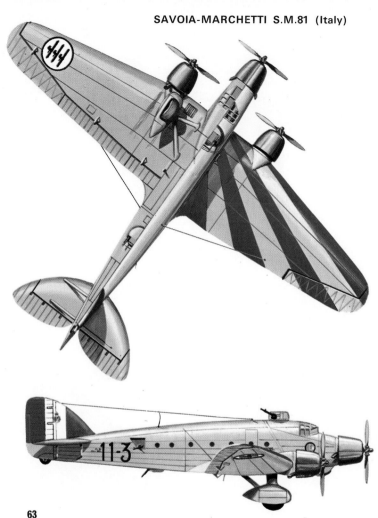

63

Savoia-Marchetti S.M.81 of the 11° *Squadriglia, 28° Gruppo, 8° Stormo B.T.* of
the *Regia Aeronautica,* Italy 1936. *Engines:* Three 670 hp Piaggio P.X RC 35
9-cylinder radials. *Span:* 78 ft 9 in. (24·00 m). *Length:* 58 ft 4¾ in. (17·80 m).
Height: 14 ft 7¼ in. (4·45 m). *Take-off weight:* 20,503 lb (9,300 kg). *Maximum
speed:* 211 mph (340 km/hr) at 3,281 ft (1,000 m). *Operational ceiling:*
22,966 ft (7,000 m). *Maximum range:* 1,243 miles (2,000 km). *Armament:*
Five 7·7 mm machine-guns, two each in dorsal and ventral turrets and one
amidships to fire laterally on either side; up to 4,409 lb (2,000 kg) of bombs
internally.

FOKKER F.VIIb-3m (Netherlands)

64

Spanish-built Fokker F.VIIb-3m/M of *Grupo* 20 of the Spanish Air Force, North Africa *ca* 1934–35. *Engines:* Three 325 hp Wright R-975 Whirlwind 9-cylinder radials. *Span:* 71 ft 2¼ in. (21·70 m). *Length:* 47 ft 8¾ in. (14·55 m). *Height:* 12 ft 9½ in. (3·90 m). *Take-off weight:* 11,442 lb (5,190 kg). *Maximum speed:* 129 mph (207 km/hr) at 9,843 ft (3,000 m). *Operational ceiling:* 10,171 ft (3,100 m). *Range:* 528 miles (850 km). *Armament:* Two 7·7 mm machine-guns, one each in dorsal and ventral positions; up to 2,205 lb (1,000 kg) of bombs.

TUPOLEV TB-3 (U.S.S.R.)

65

Tupolev TB-3 (ANT-6) of the Soviet Air Force, *ca* 1933–34. *Engines:* Four 730 hp M-17F 12-cylinder Vee type. *Span:* 129 ft 7 in. (39·494 m). *Length:* 80 ft 0½ in. (24·40 m). *Height (tail up):* 27 ft 8¾ in. (8·45 m). *Take-off weight:* 38,360 lb (17,400 kg). *Maximum speed:* 122 mph (197 km/hr) at sea level. *Operational ceiling:* 12,467 ft (3,800 m). *Range:* 839 miles (1,350 km). *Armament:* Six 7·62 mm DA-2 machine-guns, two in nose and two pairs in dorsal station; up to 4,850 lb (2,200 kg) of bombs internally and externally.

FARMAN 222 (France)

66

Farman 222.2 Bn5 of the 3e *Escadrille*, GB II/15 of the *Armée de l'Air*, Reims-Courcy 1938–39. *Engines:* Four 860 hp Gnome-Rhône 14 Kdrs 14-cylinder radials, tandem-mounted in pairs. *Span:* 118 ft 1¼ in. (36·00 m). *Length:* 70 ft 4½ in. (21·45 m). *Height:* 17 ft 0½ in. (5·20 m). *Maximum take-off weight:* 41,226 lb (18,700 kg). *Maximum speed:* 202 mph (325 km/hr) at 13,123 ft (4,000 m). *Absolute ceiling:* 27,887 ft (8,500 m). *Normal range:* 932 miles (1,500 km). *Armament:* Three 7·5 mm MAC 1934 machine-guns, one each in nose, dorsal and ventral positions; up to 9,259 lb (4,200 kg) of bombs internally.

BOEING B-17 (U.S.A.)

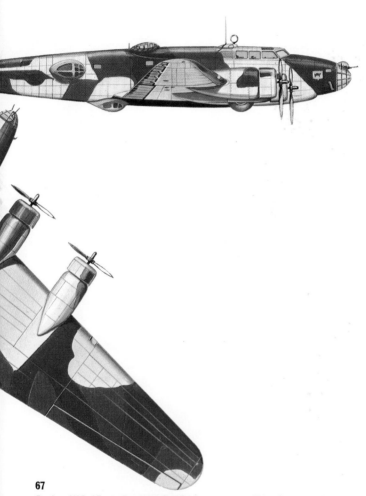

67

Boeing Y1B-17 service test aircraft, in temporary 'War Games' colours *ca* mid-1938. *Data apply to B-17B initial production version. Engines:* Four 1,200 hp Wright R-1820-51 Cyclone 9-cylinder radials. *Span:* 103 ft 9 in. (31·62 m). *Length:* 67 ft 11 in. (20·70 m). *Height:* 15 ft 5 in. (4·70 m). *Normal take-off weight:* 37,997 lb (17,235 kg). *Maximum speed:* 292 mph (470 km/hr) at 25,000 ft (7,620 m). *Operational ceiling:* 36,000 ft (10,973 m). *Normal range:* 2,400 miles (3,862 km). *Armament:* Five 0·30 in. machine-guns, one each in nose, dorsal, ventral and two waist positions; 8,000 lb (3,629 kg) of bombs internally.

LOENING OL-9 (U.S.A.)

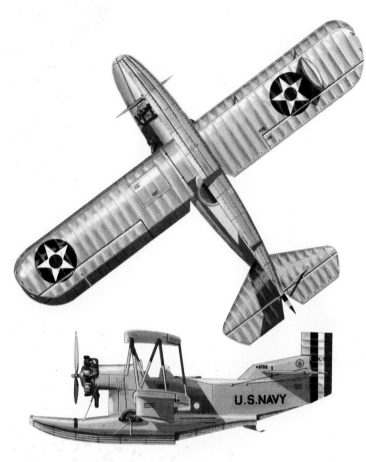

68
Loening OL-9 of the Naval Academy, US Navy, *ca* 1927–28. *Engine:* One 450 hp Pratt & Whitney R-1340-4 Wasp 9-cylinder radial. *Span:* 45 ft 0 in. (13·72 m). *Length:* 34 ft 9 in. (10·59 m). *Height:* 12 ft 9 in. (3·89 m). *Take-off weight:* 5,404 lb (2,451 kg). *Maximum speed:* 122 mph (196 km/hr) at sea level. *Operational ceiling:* 14,300 ft (4,359 m). *Range:* 625 miles (1,006 km). *Armament:* None.

69

Grumman J2F-2 Duck of the US Coast Guard, *ca* 1938–39. *Engine:* One 750 hp Wright R-1820-20 Cyclone 9-cylinder radial. *Span:* 39 ft 0 in. (11·89 m). *Length:* 34 ft 0 in. (10·36 m). *Height:* 12 ft 4 in. (3·76 m). *Take-off weight:* 6,170 lb (2,799 kg). *Maximum speed:* 180 mph (290 km/hr) at 10,000 ft (3,048 m). *Operational ceiling:* 21,000 ft (6,401 m). *Range:* 780 miles (1,255 km). *Armament:* None.

NAKAJIMA E8N (Japan)

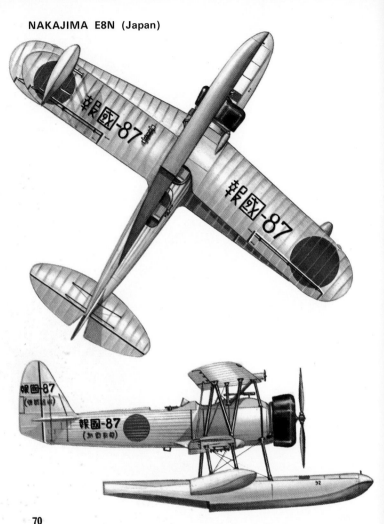

70

Nakajima E8N1 in markings denoting donation to the JNAF, *ca* 1935–36.
Engine: One 580 hp Nakajima Kotobuki 9-cylinder radial. *Span:* 36 ft 0¼ in.
(10·98 m). *Length:* 28 ft 10¾ in. (8·81 m). *Height:* 12 ft 7¼ in. (3·84 m). *Take-
off weight:* 4,189 lb (1,900 kg). *Maximum speed:* 186 mph (300 km/hr) at
9,843 ft (3,000 m). *Operational ceiling:* 23,852 ft (7,270 m). *Range:* 485
miles (780 km). *Armament:* One 7·7 mm machine-gun in forward fuselage
and (optionally) one in rear cockpit; provision for small bombs beneath lower
wings.

1 Boeing/de Havilland DH-4

The D.H.4 was a high-speed, 2-seat day bomber, designed in Britain by Geoffrey de Havilland's Aircraft Manufacturing Co and flown for the first time in August 1916. Its wartime production and career with the RAF and its predecessors are detailed in the *Bombers 1914–39* volume in this series. By wartime standards the output of British-built D.H.4's was substantial enough, but plans were laid for American production of the aircraft on a scale that was then unprecedented, involving the manufacture of well over twelve thousand examples. The Armistice of November 1918 brought an extensive curtailment of these plans, but even so the number of American-built examples (known as DH-4A's) actually built by 1919 reached four thousand eight hundred and forty-six. Two hundred and eighty-three were transferred to the U.S. Navy and Marine Corps after World War 1. The Americans were never happy with the DH-4A: it was semi-obsolete by the time it entered U.S. service, and had to be considerably redesigned and renovated to suit it to American production methods. The improved DH-4B was ready too late (October 1918) to replace it in France, but during the 1920s a considerable building and conversion programme (of DH-4A's) kept the DH-4B, DH-4M and other variants in service until 1932. The major improvement introduced by the DH-4B was to transpose the main fuel tank and the front cockpit, thus bringing the crew members close together for easier communication and, at the same time, reducing the vulnerability of the fuel system itself. The Aeromarine, Gallaudet, LWF and Thomas-Morse factories carried out one thousand five hundred and thirty-eight conversions into DH-4B's by 1926, and others were effected by various USAAS depots. There were many variants and sub-types of the DH-4B, for a multitude of duties that included ambulance, communications, dual-control training and photographic reconnaissance. Many others were utilised as test-beds for a variety of Liberty, Packard and other engines and miscellaneous equipment. In 1923 the next major version appeared as the DH-4M, the suffix letter signifying 'Modernised'. The principal innovation was the use of a steel-tube fuselage structure, increasing the empty and loaded weights, and the DH-4M was powered by a Liberty 12A engine. With this model, production was resumed, one hundred and fifty DH-4M's and DH-4M-1's being ordered from Boeing for the Army and thirty with an O2B-1 designation for the U.S. Marine Corps. Six others were completed for Cuba. In the following year an additional one hundred and thirty-five, designated DH-4M-2, were ordered from Atlantic Aircraft Corporation, the American factory of Anthony Fokker. The various DH-4B and DH-4M models continued to serve with observation and bombing squadrons until 1928, and with training and communications units for another four years after this.

2 Letov Sm-1

The Sm-1 the first product of the Vojenska Tovarna Na Letadla (Letov) company which was created from the former Czechoslovak Military Air Arsenal on 1 November 1918. Much of the former Austro-Hungarian empire lay in the new constituent Czechoslovak states of Bohemia and Moravia, and it was natural that the primary work undertaken by the Czech organisations up to mid-1919 was to repair and overhaul aircraft of the former Austro-Hungarian Air Service. However, in late 1919/early 1920 the Letov company embarked upon its first original product, the Sm-1. First flown in April 1920, the Sm-1 was designed by Alois Smolik, and was a 2-seat reconnaissance and light bombing biplane with a semi-monocoque fuselage built and covered in plywood. The wings and tail unit were built of wood, with fabric covering, and the result was a robust aeroplane, armed with three machine-guns and capable of carrying quite a reasonable bomb load. The powerplant was of war-time date, the standard unit being the Austrian Hiero Type L engine, with which the service designation was SH 1. As an alternative installation, the German Maybach Mb.IVa engine of 260 hp could be fitted, the designation in this case becoming SM 1. A variant with Maybach engine and a slightly reduced wing span was produced by the Aero factory in Czechoslovakia; this was known as the S-2, and one of these aircraft survives today in the possession of the Technical Museum in Prague. A total of ninety Sm-1 and S-2 aircraft were completed, and were the first military aircraft of national design to be built in Czechoslovakia.

3 Aero A 11

The Aero company (Aero Tovarna Letadel Dr Kabes) was one of three founder-companies of an aircraft industry in Czechoslovakia following the creation of the new Eastern European state on 28 October 1918. All began with an inheritance of work from the former Austro-Hungarian aircraft industry, and in the case of Aero this took the form of manufacturing the Austrian Phönix (Brandenburg) fighter for the new Czechoslovak Air Force. Among Aero's earliest products of its own design was the A 11, a 2-seat general-purpose biplane that first appeared in 1923 and eventually replaced the Letov Sm-1 and S-2 in Czechoslovak service. Four hundred and forty were built, serving throughout the 1920s, and proof that the A 11 really was a general-purpose aeroplane lies in the fact that no less than twenty-two different variants were included in this total. A feature of the A 11's design, which had been headed by engineer Husnik, was that a wide variety of powerplants could be interchanged with ease in the basic airframe. The A 11 was developed from the Maybach-engined A 12 which first flew in 1923 and of which ninety-three examples were built in 1924–25. It generally resembled the A 12 except in its powerplant, which in the original A 11 model was the

240 hp Walter W-IV, a licence-built version of the German BMW IV. The principal model was the standard A 11, with its A 11N night reconnaissance counterpart, both powered by the W-IV engine. The Ab 11 and Ab 11N were bomber variants, powered by the 240 hp Brietfeld-Danek Perun II engine, while the daytime A 25 and A 125, and nocturnal A 21, were produced for training duties. The A 29 target tug of 1926, nine of which were completed, was a twin-float version, the first-ever Czechoslovak seaplane. Other engines to be installed in the basic A 11 airframe included the 300 hp Hispano-Suiza 8 Fb (A 11HS), the Lorraine Dietrich (A 11LD), the 420 hp Bristol Jupiter (A 11J), the 600 hp Skoda L (A 11C) and the 240 hp Walter Castor. Eight A 11HS's were sold to Finland in 1927.

4 Polikarpov R-5

In production and service for the greater part of a decade following its first appearance in 1928, the R-5 was probably the most widely built and certainly one of the most widely used reconnaissance-bomber/general-purpose aeroplanes to appear during the years between the two world wars. It was a contemporary of such other European types as the Fokker C.V, Potez 25 and Westland Wapiti, and is claimed to have been better than all of them. Some six thousand R-5's are thought to have been built, in a multitude of variants for almost every conceivable military and civil task. The R-5 successfully

completed its state acceptance trials in 1930, and entered production later that year, initially in the capacity of a *razvedchik* or reconnaissance-bomber aircraft, powered by a 500 hp M-17B Vee-type engine. This was followed in 1931 by a *shturmovik* (assault) version, carrying a 1,102 lb (500 kg) bomb load and heavily armed with five forward-firing 7·62 mm PV-1 machine-guns plus two DP guns of similar calibre mounted in the rear cockpit. Two new models, powered by M-17F engines, appeared in 1933. One of these was the R-5S reconnaissance-bomber, with streamlined wheel fairings and other detailed improvements; the other was the single-seat R-5T torpedo-carrying version, fifty of which were built during 1935 for the Soviet Naval Air Service. Another naval version, for reconnaissance, was the R-5a or MR-5, a twin-float seaplane with increased fin area and M-17B engine. All versions could equally easily be fitted with a ski landing gear. Large numbers of R-5's were also built for Aeroflot, many of them with enclosed front cockpits and a small passenger cabin in an enlarged rear fuselage. Others served in the ambulance and training roles both with Aeroflot and with the Soviet military services. Polikarpov R-5's saw operational service in two quarters during the latter half of the 1930s. In the Spanish Civil War those flying in support of the Republican forces were nicknamed 'Natasha'; other R-5's were engaged in combat against Japanese aircraft in the clashes in Mongolia in 1938–39. Many remained in service after the outbreak of World War 2 and were encountered particularly during the 'winter war' with Finland of 1939–40.

5 Breguet XIX

Designed to replace the successful Breguet XIV wartime bomber (see *Bombers 1914–19*), the Breguet Type XIX was evolved in 1921 and made its first public appearance as an exhibit at the *Salon de l'Aéronautique* in Paris later that year. At that time it had not yet flown; it made its maiden flight in May 1922, powered by a 420 hp Renault engine, which was later exchanged first for a 375 hp and then for a 450 hp Lorraine Vee-type engine. The Breguet XIX was of robust metal construction, with fabric covering, and its clean lines and single-strut sesquiplane layout made it straightforward to build and to maintain. A feature of the design was the ease with which a large variety of powerplants could be fitted. During its fifteen-year operational life the Breguet XIX was powered by 400 and 450 hp Lorraine, 420 or 480 hp Jupiter, 480, 500 or 550 hp Renault, 450 or 500 hp Hispano-Suiza, 500 hp Farman and 500 hp Salmson engines. A twin-float landing gear could be substituted for the more usual landplane undercarriage. French production, which began in 1925, reached about one thousand one hundred examples, and at its peak was turning out Breguet XIX's at the rate of four aircraft a day. Despite a multiplicity of variants,

created by the many permutations of powerplant, landing gear, armament and detail features, there were only three basic functional versions of the aircraft. These were the XIXA.2 (2-seat observation/reconnaissance), the XIXB.2 (2-seat day and night bomber) and the XIX GR (*grande reconnaissance*). All three served with the French *Aviation Militaire*, and substantial exports of A.2 and B.2 models were made to Argentina, Belgium, Bolivia, China, Greece, Iran (Persia), Poland, Rumania and Yugoslavia. In addition, the Breguet XIX was built under licence in Belgium (approximately one hundred and fifty by SABCA), Greece, Japan, Spain (one hundred and three by CASA) and by Ikarus in Yugoslavia. The Breguets began to disappear from first-line French bomber squadrons in the latter 1930s, although one hundred and sixteen were still on charge at 1 January 1936. Some of the foreign users of the aircraft kept them in service until at least 1940. Individual Breguet XIX's were responsible for a considerable number of endurance and other record flights during the 1920s and 1930s. Among these, perhaps the most noteworthy was the record-breaking *Point d'Interrogation* (Question Mark), which was flown by the Frenchmen Dieudonné, Costes and Maurice Bellonte on the first successful east-to-west air crossing of the North Atlantic, from Paris to New York, on 1–2 September 1930. Another famous Breguet XIX, the *Nungesser et Coli*, is currently in the possession of the Musée de l'Air near Paris.

6 Kawasaki Army Type 88

The Kawasaki Aircraft Engineering Co originated as the Aviation Department of the Kawasaki Dockyard Co, which first began the manufacture of aircraft by building French Salmson biplanes and their engines under licence for the Japanese Army Air Force after World War 1. In 1923 the German Dr Richard Vogt (later of Blohm und Voss) became chief designer for Kawasaki, and he was responsible for designing a 2-seat reconnaissance biplane to an Army specification issued in March 1925. The three prototypes of this aircraft were known as KDA-2 (Kawasaki Dockyard Army type number 2), and the first was completed in February 1927. Performance during flight tests in the next few months included a level speed of 149 mph (240 km/hr) and a time of 20 minutes to climb to 16,404 ft (5,000 m), and in August 1927 the design received official Army acceptance. Production was initiated in February 1928 as the Army Type 88-I, the powerplant being a Japanese-built version of the German BMW VI Vee-type engine. The basic design was also utilised to perform as a light bomber, with racks for small weapons fitted beneath the lower wings and somewhat improved engine cowling lines. This version was designated Type 88-II. Operations during some ten years in Japanese Army service included participation in the 'Shanghai Inci-dent' of 1932 and in Tsinan and Manchuria. Five hundred and twenty Type 88's were manufac-tured by the parent company in 1928–31; in addition, the Army Arsenal at Tachikawa completed a further one hundred and eighty-seven.

7 Mitsubishi B2M

The first aeroplane evolved in Japan for the torpedo attack role was the Mitsubishi B1M, which was designed in 1922 by a Mitsubishi team under Herbert Smith, formerly of the British Sopwith company. It flew for the first time in January 1923, and remained in production until 1933, by which time a total of four hundred and forty-two had been built for the Naval Air Force. They appeared in three principal models and were powered by either Napier Lion or Hispano-Suiza engines of 450 hp. Official designa-tion of the B1M was Navy Type 13, the figure indicating the thirteenth year of the reign of Emperor Taisho, in 1923. In 1927 the Japanese Army Air Force adopted a modified Hispano-engined version, of which forty-eight were completed. These, under an amended designation system, were known as Type 87, indicating year 2587 in the Japanese calendar, or AD 1927. In February 1928 the JNAF issued a requirement for a new metal-structure torpedo-bomber-reconnaissance aircraft to replace the B1M and three designs by British teams were called for by Mitsubishi: the 3MR3 by Herbert Smith's team, with 650 hp Arm-strong Siddeley Leopard engine;

the Blackburn 3MR4 (600 hp Hispano-Suiza); and the Handley Page 3MR5 (650 hp Hispano-Suiza). Only the Blackburn design was actually submitted to the JNAF, and this was accepted in 1929. Blackburn completed the first prototype in the U.K., delivering it to Japan in February 1930 and sending its chief engineer, G. E. Petty, to supervise the construction of further examples. Three more prototypes were built in Japan, of which the last, incorporating several modifications, ultimately produced the performance required of the new aeroplane. It entered production in March 1932 with the Mitsubishi designation B2M1 and the official Navy designation Type 89 Model 1. Major modifications introduced in 1934, to improve upon the somewhat poor serviceability of the aircraft, resulted in the Model 2 or B2M2. When production ended in 1935 a total of two hundred and four B2M1/B2M2's (excluding prototypes) had been manufactured.

8 Fairey Fox

In the mid-1920s two aeroplanes, more than any others, produced a profound effect upon British official requirements for combat aircraft; for, although both were evolved as single-engined day bombers, they were appreciably faster than any of the standard fighters then in RAF service. The Hawker Hart, described separately, was ultimately the more successful type, but it was preceded more than three years earlier by the Fairey Fox, whose prototype (J7941) flew for the first

time on 3 January 1925. It owed its existence to the perspicacity of Richard Fairey who, during a visit to the U.S.A. in 1923, had recognised the advantages of the Curtiss D-12 engine and took steps to obtain it for use in a British aircraft. The Fox, with the low-drag American engine installed and every other effort made to streamline its appearance, thus appeared as an extremely clean design aerodynamically. It was 50 mph (80 km/hr) faster than its predecessor, the Fairey Fawn (which first flew only a year before the Fox), and could show a clean pair of heels to any current RAF fighter. So impressed was Air Chief Marshal Sir Hugh Trenchard, when the Fox was demonstrated before him in October 1925, that immediately he ordered a complete squadron of the type. These were delivered from August 1926 to No 12 Squadron, which later adopted a fox's head as the squadron emblem. It was the only RAF fighter unit to operate the Fox, only twenty-eight of which were built because of budgetary restrictions. Some of these later became Mk IA's when refitted with Rolls-Royce Kestrel engines. They remained in RAF service until 1934, latterly with the Special Duty Flight at Boscombe Down. An all-metal prototype (J9834) was built as the Fox IIM to Specification 12/26, but in competitive trials with the Hart and the Avro Antelope the Hawker design was chosen for future RAF production. However, Fairey set up a daughter company, Avions Fairey, in Belgium in September 1931 to build a private-venture fighter (the

Firefly) which also utilised the Kestrel engine. Firefly production for the Belgian *Aéronautique Militaire* was followed in 1933 by the manufacture of twenty-eight Fox II's and sixty-eight Fox III's for the Belgian air force. It was then decided, in an attempt to update the Fox's performance, to re-engine the design with the 860 hp Hispano-Suiza 12 Ydrs engine, to install a covered enclosure over the two cockpits and to add streamlined fairings over the main undercarriage wheels. In this form the aircraft was redesignated Fox VI; seventy-six of these were completed, comprising fifty-two Fox VIC fighters and twenty-four Fox VIR reconnaissance aircraft. Fox production ended in 1939 after the completion of two examples of the single-seat Fox VII (or 'Mono Fox') and fifteen Fox VIII's, bringing overall Belgian manufacture to a total of one hundred and eighty-nine.

9 Hawker Hind

The Hind was essentially an interim replacement type for the Hart day bomber (*q.v.*), and as such its design was based substantially upon that of its predecessor. It was evolved to Specification G. 7/34 to equip newly-formed bomber squadrons under the RAF expansion scheme pending the arrival of more modern monoplane types such as the Fairey Battle. Although retaining a close general resemblance to the Hart, the Hind introduced a number of design improvements including the adoption of the Rolls-Royce Kestrel

V engine and redesign of the observer's cockpit and gun installation. The prototype (K2915) was a converted Hart airframe, flying for the first time in its new configuration on 12 September 1934. The first of an initial order for twenty Hinds was flown just less than a year later, and deliveries began late in 1935 to Nos 18, 21 and 34 squadrons. Eventual production of the Hind totalled five hundred and ninety-two (all Hawker-built), including sales to Afghanistan (twenty), Eire (six), Kenya (six), Latvia (three), New Zealand (approx. thirty), Persia (thirty-five), South Africa (approx. twenty-two), Switzerland (one) and Yugoslavia (three). At home, Hinds served with no less than twenty-five RAF bomber squadrons (Nos 12, 15, 18, 21, 34, 40, 49, 50, 52, 57, 63, 83, 88, 90, 98, 103, 104, 106, 107, 108, 113, 114, 139, 142 and 211) until 1938 and later with eleven squadrons of the Auxiliary Air Force, latterly in a training role.

10 Fairey Gordon and Seal

Gordon and Seal were, respectively, the RAF and Fleet Air Arm names for the aircraft produced to replace the Fairey IIIF in the two British services. Both were, in essence, further developments of the aircraft which they replaced, the Gordon prototype (J9154) being converted from a IIIF Mk IVB and that for the Seal (S1325) from a IIIF Mk IIIB. Both prototypes first flew in 1930, and on 29 September 1932 the Seal prototype made another 'first' flight, this time in seaplane configuration with a twin-float landing gear. The two types differed from the Fairey IIIF principally in the substitution of an Armstrong Siddeley Panther two-row radial engine for their predecessor's Napier Lion. The initial production Gordon Mk I retained more or less unchanged the distinctive tail design of the Fairey IIIF, but new, more rounded vertical surfaces were designed for the Seal, and these were also introduced on the Gordon II together with such other refinements as Frise-type ailerons. Twenty-four Gordon II's were built to RAF orders, to Specification 14/33, compared with one hundred and fifty-four Mk I's to Specification 18/30; in addition, it is believed that about thirty more were produced by conversion of Fairey IIIF's. The first Gordons entered service with No 40 Squadron at Upper Heyford in the spring of 1931, and the aircraft later served with Nos 35 and 207 Squadrons in the U.K. and Nos 6, 14, 45 and 47 in the Middle East and Africa. Thirteen Gordon I's and an equal number of Gordon II's were allocated to the Royal New Zealand Air Force, and small numbers were sold to Brazil, Egypt and Peru. Production of the Seal amounted to ninety aircraft, the first of which were delivered in April 1933 to Nos 820 and 821 Squadrons of the FAA, embarking later that year in HMS *Courageous*. Other naval squadrons to re-equip with Seals during 1934–35 included No 822 (*Furious*), 823 (*Glorious*), 824 (*Hermes*, later *Eagle*) and 825. They were gradually withdrawn between 1935–38 in favour of the Blackburn Shark; by this time the Gordon also had been retired from first-line service with the RAF, although it continued to be used for some time afterwards in a target-towing role.

11 **Westland Wapiti and Wallace**

No less than seven British aircraft manufactures sent prototypes to Martlesham Heath in 1927 in a bid to secure orders for an RAF replacement for the war-vintage D.H.9A day bomber. The Air Ministry requirement had specified the maximum possible use of D.H.9A components, and Westland, which had participated in production of the de Havilland design, thus had a distinct advantage. The Westland prototype (J8495) retained, virtually without alteration, the entire wing cellule and landing gear of its de Havilland ancestor, allied to an entirely new-design fuselage and a 420 hp Bristol Jupiter VI radial engine; it made its first flight early in 1927. In December of that year an initial order was placed for twenty-five Wapiti Mk I for service trials with No 84 Squadron in Iraq. These had fabric-covered wooden wings and rear fuselages, but the Jupiter VI-engined Mk II (ten built) introduced an all-metal basic structure which became standard for all subsequent models. Major production version was the Mk IIA, with 550 hp Jupiter VIIIF engine; four hundred and fifteen were built to RAF contracts. Thirty-five examples were built of the 'long-fuselage' Mk V – though in fact the length of this version was that originally intended for *all* versions of the Wapiti, but not adopted due to an oversight in the early detail design. Final RAF version was the Mk VI, sixteen of which were built for instructional duties and fitted with dual controls. Wapitis served as general-purpose aircraft with Nos 5, 11, 20, 27, 28, 31, 39 and 60 Squadrons in India and Nos 30, 55 and 84 Squadrons in Iraq, and later with several Auxiliary Air Force squadrons in the U.K. Total production to Air Ministry contracts, including prototypes, reached five hundred and seventeen. Of these, twenty-five Mk IIA's were allocated to the Royal Canadian Air Force, six to the Royal Australian Air Force and four to the South African Air Force. Four others were sold to the Kwangsi government in China, four to the monarchy of Hedjaz in Saudi Arabia, and twenty-four to Australia. A further twenty-seven were built under licence in South Africa by the Aircraft and Artillery Depot. Approximately fifty of the aircraft ordered as Wapiti IIA's were converted to (or completed as) Westland Wallace Mk I's. The Wallace originated as a private-venture Westland development (P.V.6) of the Wapiti with a Pegasus engine, the 'long' fuselage of the Wapiti V and improvements to the landing gear. In addition to the Wapiti conversions, eight Mk I and one hundred and four Mk II Wallaces were ordered as such. The Mk II introduced a higher powered engine (the 680 hp Pegasus IV) and fully-enclosed accommodation for the 2-man crew, including a 'lobster-back' transparent shield for the observer/gunner. The Wallace served only with Auxiliary squadrons, latterly on target-towing duties, some surviving until as late as 1943. One Wallace and another Wapiti-Wallace derivative, the Westland P.V.3., were specially modified in 1932, both being re-engined with 525 hp Pegasus IS.3 engines. On 3 April 1933 they made the first aeroplane flights above the earth's highest point, the 29,028 ft (8,848 m) summit of Mount Everest in the Himalayas, repeating their feat sixteen days later.

12 **Polikarpov U-2 (Po-2)**

One of the most extensively-produced general-purpose aircraft of any era, the Polikarpov U-2, first appeared in the late 1920s. Some twenty thousand were built up to 1952, before production ended; it was active throughout World War 2 and is still in fairly extensive use today in the U.S.S.R. and Soviet bloc countries. Separate production was initiated in Poland from 1948–54, under the designations CSS-13 (for agricultural work) and CSS-S-13, and during its forty-year life the aircraft has been used by both civil and military organisations for observation, light bombing, transport, ambulance, liaison, supply-dropping, forestry patrol, training and many other miscellaneous duties. The U-2 was designed in 1927 as a 2-seat primary trainer, flying for the first time on 7 January 1928. Up to 1941 (by which time production had reached some thirteen and a half thousand) it was employed primarily for this purpose or for other non-aggressive duties. All main Soviet production models were powered by the 100 hp M-11, a five-cylinder radial engine, manufacture beginning in 1928. The U-2 was introduced to more belligerent roles after the outbreak of World War 2, when it was widely used by day and night as a close-support aircraft or 'nuisance' raider. In this capacity it was designated U-2VS (*Voyskovaya Serya* = Military Series), was armed with a 7·62 mm ShKAS machine-gun in the rear cockpit and could carry up to 550 lb (250 kg) of small bombs on racks beneath the lower wings. The U-2VS equipped literally dozens of Soviet night bomber regiments in World War 2, was prominent in the defence of Stalingrad in 1942, and by the end of the war was operating with rocket projectiles as an alternative to the underwing bomb load. The U-2 was equally widely used in the transport role (including an enclosed-cabin version known as the U-2ShS, seating four passengers) and as the U-2NAK artillery night-spotting aircraft. The designation Po-2, indicating personally the name of its designer, Nikolai Polikarpov, was awarded officially after his death in 1944 as a joint tribute to a highly-respected aeroplane and a gifted and prolific designer.

13 Fokker C.V

One of the most popular and versatile aircraft of the 1919–39 period, the C.V light bomber and reconnaissance biplane, was probably the single most successful military type ever produced by the Dutch Fokker company. Its career spanned three-quarters of the two inter-war decades, during which time it served with the air forces of almost a dozen countries. Its flying qualities were excellent, and its simplicity of maintenance endeared it as much to its ground staffs as to the men who flew in it. Indeed, so reliable was the C.V that for several years – while orders for production of other types of Fokker aircraft were either small or non-existent – there was a severe shortage of work at the Fokker factories because so few C.V's needed to be returned for modification or overhaul. The design was based upon the earlier Fokker C.IV, and first flew in prototype form in May 1924. To make the aircraft adaptable to a wide range of military duties, Fokker evolved the ingenious solution of offering the C.V with several alternative sets of wings, each interchangeable for one of the other sets in less than an hour; a selection of alternative powerplants could also be interchanged with similar facility. The first three production models had constant-chord upper and lower wings, braced by N-pattern interplane struts and bearing balanced ailerons on the upper mainplane. These wings came in three sizes, with gross areas of 403·6, 439·2 and 496·2 sq ft (37·5, 40·8 and 46·1 sq m), the aircraft's designation being C.V-A, C.V-B or C.V-C respectively. BMW, Hispano-

Suiza or Lorraine-Dietrich Vee-type engines could be installed in any of the three models; some C.V-A's were fitted with 420 hp Liberty engines. These early variants were built in limited numbers for the Dutch *Luchtvaartafdeling* (LVA) and for export. A major change in wing configuration was then introduced in production from 1926, the arrangement being almost of a sesquiplane nature with a much smaller lower wing. Both wings were tapered in plan, with rounded tips and tapered, non-overhanging ailerons on the upper wings. Only two sized sets of wings in this form were utilised, identifying respectively the C.V-D and C.V-E. The C.V-D had wings of 310·0 sq ft (28·8 sq m) gross area, braced by V-struts; while the C.V-E retained the more common N-struts but with the wing area increased to 423·0 sq ft (39·3 sq m). The fuselage remained virtually unchanged, but the range of powerplants was extended to include a number of radial engines such as the Armstrong Siddeley Jaguar, Bristol Jupiter or Pegasus and Pratt & Whitney Hornet or Wasp, as well as later Vee-type units such as the Rolls-Royce Kestrel. Sixty-seven C.V-D's, with Hispano-Suiza or Jaguar engines originally, were delivered to the LVA, which designated them C.VI in service; most were subsequently re-engined with Kestrels. Thirty-four were still in service when Holland was invaded in May 1940. The Dutch MLD (Naval Air Service) received six C.V-C floatplanes and eighteen C.V-E landplanes, and a further twenty C.V-E's, with 400 hp Napier Lion engines, were operated by the Netherlands Indies Air Force. Denmark purchased five C.V-B's and one C.V-E, also building thirteen of the former and thirty of the latter version under licence. Several C.V's of various models were sold to Finland; Hungarian factories built the C.V-D in quantity, and Jupiter-engined C.V-E's were manufactured by Meridionali in Italy as the Ro 1. The sale of five C.V-E's to Norway was followed by Norwegian production of both D and E models, about forty of which were still in service in 1940. Sweden purchased two D's and six E's, later building forty-six of these two versions in the State Aircraft Factory; they served under J 3 or S 6 *Flygvapnet* designations, except for three which were sold to Finland. The remaining foreign customer was Switzerland, who after buying three D's and three E's had fifty-eight built locally by EKW and the Altenrhein factory of Dornier. The Swiss EKW C-35 (see *Fighters 1919–39*) was a direct derivative of the Fokker C.V. This versatile Dutch aeroplane was involved in several endurance and other notable flights during its career, the best-known perhaps being the rescue of General Nobile from the Arctic by one of the Swedish C.V's, after his unsuccessful attempt to reach the North Pole in the airship *Italia*.

14 Vought Corsair series

The name Corsair achieved worldwide renown through the exploits of Chance Vought's famous gull-winged World War 2 fighter, but more than a dozen years before its appearance other Vought Corsairs had formed an entire family of naval observation and scouting biplanes produced in a veritable profusion of variants, not only for the U.S. Navy and Marine Corps but for export to nearly a dozen other countries. The design, based upon the Pratt & Whitney Wasp radial engine and featuring an all-metal fuselage structure, originated in 1926, when two O2U-1 prototypes were ordered for evaluation. Delivery of a hundred and thirty production O2U-1 Corsairs to the USN and USMC began in the following year. These were open-cockpit 2-seaters, carrying two guns and (optionally) a small bomb load, and served in landplane, floatplane and amphibian forms at shore stations or on board carriers such as the *Langley*. They were followed in 1928–29 by successive batches of thirty-seven O2U-2, eighty O2U-3 and forty-two O2U-4 Corsairs, differing chiefly in tail design and lesser details. One O2U-3 was evaluated by the U.S. Army (designation O-28), but no orders resulted. Chance Vought's next development was the O3U-1 amphibian, basically an improved O2U-4 with increased wing sweepback, of which eighty-seven were delivered from 1930 for shipboard service. Twenty-nine examples followed of the O3U-2 (600 hp Hornet cowled engine, redesigned fin and landing gear); this model, for the Marine Corps, was redesignated SU-1 in service to denote its primary function of scout biplane. The Wasp-engined O3U-3 (seventy-six built) introduced an enlarged and more rounded rudder, and was followed by sixty-four Hornet-powered O3U-4 (SU-2 and SU-3) aircraft. The XSU-4 represented a much-modernised version, featuring a long-chord NACA-type engine cowling, further enlargement of the tail surfaces and fully-enclosed crew accommodation; the old-style narrow cowling was, however, retained on the forty series-built SU-4's. The XO3U-5 did not go into production, but a prototype and thirty-two production O3U-6's for the Marine Corps were built in 1935. When America entered World War 2 there were a hundred and forty-one Corsairs of different types on Navy strength, although by this time they were no longer in first-line service. The Corsair design also yielded a number of export variants, most of them with one or another variant of the Hornet engine. Model V-65's, corresponding broadly to the O2U-1, were built for the Argentine Naval Air Service, Brazil Army Air Service, and the air forces of China, Mexico and Peru. Mexican factories built Corsairs under licence after purchasing ten from the U.S.A., and licence production of the V-935 model was undertaken in Thailand, where seventy-two were built. A lower-powered version was the V-100 Corsair Junior, suitable for primary or specialised advanced training or general-purpose duties. Variants with Twin Wasp engines included the V-99 and V-135, the latter being a single-seat fighter model.

15 Letov S-328

Like the first indigenous product of the Czechoslovak Letov company (the Sm-1 described on page 98), the S-328 was also a design of Alois Smolik. It first began to take shape in 1931, being developed from designs known as the S-28 and its derivative, the S-228, which was supplied to the Estonian Air Force. The S-328 was designed in 1932, originally to meet a Finnish requirement. The first prototype, designated S-328F, was powered by a 580 hp Bristol Pegasus IIM.2 radial engine and armed with two forward- and two rearward-firing machine-guns. The Finnish Air Force did not after all order the type, but after Hitler's coming to power in Germany in 1933 the Czechoslovak Ministry of National Defence took a closer interest in the Letov reconnaissance-bomber, deciding in 1934 to place the aircraft in production as a replacement for the ageing Aero A 11. Manufacture was still in progress when the *Wehrmacht* invaded Bohemia and Moravia in March 1939, and continued until a total of four hundred and forty-five S-328's had been built. Variants included thirteen S-328N night fighters, with a total of six machine-guns, and four S-328V floatplanes, mounted on a twin-float gear designed and built by Shorts in the U.K. A prototype was completed of the S-428, which had a 650 hp Avia-built Hispano-Suiza 12 Nbr Vee-type engine, and Letov also

built six examples of the S-528, similar to the standard S-328 but with an 800 hp Gnome-Rhône Mistral Major radial engine in a long-chord NACA-type cowling. After the German occupation, the Letov biplanes were seized by the *Luftwaffe*, which employed large numbers of them in a training role and transferred others to the German-sponsored Slovak Air Force and to the Bulgarian Air Force. An active part was taken in the war by the Slovak S-328's, which supported the *Luftwaffe* in reconnaissance and bombing sorties during the early advances into Poland and the Soviet Union. The Bulgarian machines served mainly on coastal patrol duties in the Black Sea area.

16 Fairey Swordfish

The Fairey Aviation Co already had a long-established tradition of building sea-going aircraft when, in 1932, it began as a private venture the design of a new torpedo/spotter/reconnaissance biplane known as the T.S.R.I. This prototype (S 1533) made its first flight on 21 March 1933, but was lost some six months later after failing to pull out of a trial spin. The basic design had, however, already been proved satisfactory, and so to Air Ministry Specification S. 15/33 Fairey built a modified prototype (K4190) designated T.S.R.II. This machine, the true prototype of the later Swordfish, featured a lengthened fuselage, enlarged tail fin, redesigned landing gear and other detail improvements; it flew for the first time on 17 April 1934, and an initial production batch of eighty-six Swordfish I was ordered a year later to Specification S. 38/34. Delivery of these began in February 1936, the first FAA squadron (No 825, in HMS *Glorious*) receiving its first Swordfish in the following July. The aircraft subsequently equipped pre-war squadrons Nos 810, 811, 812, 813, 821, 823, 824 and 833 in the carriers *Ark Royal*, *Courageous*, *Eagle* and *Furious*, and in addition to normal peacetime deployment in its intended roles the Swordfish undertook a considerable burden of training work. As an alternative to the 1,610 lb (730 kg) torpedo which it was designed to carry beneath the fuselage, the Swordfish I could carry a 1,500 lb (680 kg) mine in the same position or an equivalent weight of small bombs distributed under the fuselage and lower wings. It could operate either with the more usual wheeled landing gear or in twin-float form, a configuration first test-flown on 10 November 1934. After completing six hundred and ninety-two Swordfish, including prototypes, Fairey ceased production early in 1940 in order to concentrate upon the Albacore, but manufacture of later versions was continued by Blackburn, who built one thousand six hundred and ninety-nine. Wartime career of the Swordfish is described in *Bombers 1939–45* in this series.

17 Vickers Vildebeest and Vincent

A near-contemporary of the Fleet Air Arm's Fairey Swordfish, the Vickers Vildebeest design was initiated in 1926 to provide a replacement for the RAF's Hawker Horsley torpedo-bomber. The first of two prototypes (N230) was flown for the first time in April 1928, powered by a 460 hp Bristol Jupiter VIII engine, and production Vildebeest Mk I aircraft began to be delivered (first to No 100 Squadron) in 1932. These had 600 hp Pegasus IM.3 uncowled engines, Handley Page slotted wings and a Vee-type divided-axle landing gear that permitted an 18-in torpedo to be slung directly beneath the fuselage; twenty-two were completed. There were four basic production models of the Vildebeest. The Mk II (thirty built) was powered by a 635 hp Bristol Pegasus IIM.3 uncowled engine; the Mk III (one hundred and eleven built) was generally similar except that it carried a third crew member in a remodelled rear cockpit; while the Mk IV (eighteen built) differed chiefly in having a Bristol Perseus VIII sleeve-valve engine installed in a close-fitting cowling. All versions were operable from twin-float landing gear, which could be interchanged readily with the standard wheel undercarriage. Despite the comparatively small number of Vildebeests built, they enjoyed a long service life, and two Coastal Command squadrons (Nos 36 and 100) were still equipped with these aircraft at the outbreak of World War 2, due to the belated entry into service of the twin-engined Beauforts that were to have replaced them. They were stationed in the Far East, but most of them were destroyed when the Japanese overran Singapore in 1941. A total of twenty-six Vildebeests were completed for the Spanish Naval Air Service by CASA, being fitted with 600 hp Hispano-Suiza 12 Lbr Vee-type engines which gave them a much less clumsy appearance. The original British prototype, similarly re-engined, was also sold to Spain later. Interest shown in the Vildebeest by other foreign governments did not result in any orders, but twenty-seven of the Mk III's built were supplied to the Royal New Zealand Air Force. A variation of the basic design, also with an extra cockpit for a third crew member, was the Vickers Vincent. The Vincent was produced to replace the Wapiti and Fairey IIIF in the Army co-operation and general purpose capacities overseas, a converted Vildebeest Mk I (S 1714) serving as prototype. It was powered similarly to the Mk II Vildebeest, and could carry a supplementary fuel tank under the fuselage in place of the latter's torpedo. One hundred and ninety-seven Vincents were completed, many following amendment of contracts that had originally specified Vildebeests. Vincents served with Nos 5, 27, 28 and 31 Squadrons in India and Nos 8, 45, 47, 55, 84, 207, 223 and 244 Squadrons in the Middle East and Africa from 1934 onward. Like their stablemates, a few Vincents remained in service long enough to carry out limited operations during the early years of World War 2.

18 Curtiss F8C/O2C Helldiver

To replace the American-built version of the war-vintage de Havilland DH-4 light bomber and reconnaissance aircraft in the middle and late 1920s, Curtiss evolved for the U.S. Army in 1924 a prototype aircraft known as the XO-1, powered by a Liberty engine. This was unsuccessful at first, but in 1925, after being re-engined with a Packard 1A-1500, it was rewarded with a production contract. Curtiss subsequently built one hundred and four, with Curtiss D-12 engines, under O-1 series designations, and sixty-six similar but Liberty-engined O-11's, these aircraft having the name Falcon in Army service. Between 1927 and 1930 a further one hundred and fifty-four examples of a ground attack version, designated A-3 and A-3B, were also completed for the Army. With these Army models already in production and service it was therefore logical when, in 1927, the U.S. Marine Corps also sought a DH-4 replacement, to consider adaptation of the Falcon for the purpose. The Marine Corps requirement was originally for a 2-seat fighter, with secondary capability as a light bomber and reconnaissance type, and two XF8C-1 prototypes were ordered in mid-1927. Their completion early in 1928 was followed by four F8C-1 and twenty-one F8C-3 aircraft, all of them differing from the Army Falcons principally in having a Pratt & Whitney Wasp radial engine as their powerplant. In USMC service they were later redesignated OC-1 and OC-2. Two other prototypes, the XF8C-2 and XF8C-4, appeared in 1929 and represented development of the aircraft to fulfil the role of dive-bomber. No production of the former was undertaken, but twenty-seven F8C-4's were built for Navy and Marine Corps service. They were given the name Helldiver, a name which stuck to later and quite separate Curtiss designs for naval dive-bombers. The final two F8C-4's were converted to F8C-5's by sub-stituting a different model Wasp engine, and a further sixty-one F8C-5 (later O2C-1) Helldivers were delivered from 1931.

19 IMAM (Meridionali) Ro 37

The original Officine Ferroviarie Meridionali of Naples entered the aircraft manufacturing business in 1923. In 1934 the SAI Aeronautiche Romeo was created to assume responsibility for its aviation activi-ties, and this in turn became SA Industrie Mecchaniche e Aero-nautiche Meridionali two years later. All aircraft produced by this organisation bore Ro (for Romeo) designations, and included both civil and military types. The Ro 37, which first flew in prototype form in 1934, was a 2-seat biplane designed for strategic reconnais-sance, light bombing and general-purpose duties. Both cockpits were open, the rear one having a movable machine-gun on a ring mounting, and in each side of the fuselage was a large window to facilitate obser-vation of ground objectives. Power-plant of the standard original pro-duction Ro 37 was a 550 hp Fiat

A.30 RA *bis* 12-cylinder liquid-cooled Vee-type engine. About two hundred of this version were built, making their operational debut with the *Regia Aeronautica* during the Italian mid-1930s campaigns in Ethiopia. The Ro 37 also appeared in service as a close-support air-craft flying on the side of General Franco's Nationalist forces during the Spanish Civil War. The Vee-engined Ro 37 was followed into production and service with Italian *Squadriglie da Osservazione Aerea* by the radial-engined Ro 37 *bis* (illus-trated), which was generally similar to its predecessor except for the powerplant. Two hundred and eighty-three of these aircraft, mostly of the Ro 37 *bis* version, were still in service when Italy entered World War 2 in June 1940, and continued to operate until 1943, in many different capacities, on almost every front. Those in the East African theatre, despite their age and limited manoeuvrability, were even employed in an inter-ception role. Some were exported pre-war, to Afghanistan, Ecuador, Hungary and Uruguay.

20 Curtiss SBC Helldiver

Aviation history records very few examples indeed of a biplane deve-loped from an original monoplane design, but one such was the Curtiss SBC carrier-based scout bomber, which had its origins in the parasol-winged XF12C-1 fighter proto-type produced by Curtiss to a 1932 Navy contract. It was first flown in the autumn of 1933, becoming redesignated XS4C-1 in the scout category at the end of that year and XSBC-1 for the scout-bomber role in January 1934. Dive-bombing trials in the following September proved the parasol-wing layout to be unsatisfactory and a second prototype, a biplane, was ordered in April 1935. This machine (BuAer number 9225) was designated XSBC-2 and made its first flight on 9 December 1935, being almost completely redesigned from the original fighter prototype. Its experimental two-row Whirlwind engine was later replaced by an R-1535-82 Wasp, gaining it yet another change of designation to XSBC-3, and in virtually unchanged form this was ordered into production in August 1936. The first of eighty-three SBC-3's were delivered to U.S. Navy Squadron VS-5 in July 1937; they later served also with VS-3 and VS-6, and sixty-nine were still on strength at the time of Pearl Harbor. Meanwhile, Curtiss had fitted a single-row Cyclone in the final SBC-3, which thus became the XSBC-4 and prototype for the major production version of this Helldiver family. Delivery began in March 1939 of an initial order for fifty-eight SBC-4's, and in June 1940 fifty USN Helldivers were diverted in partial fulfilment of a French order for ninety Curtiss Model 77's (export equivalent of the SBC-4). Forty-four of these were embarked in the French aircraft *Béarn*, which had sailed for France just before news of France's surrender reached America. The carrier put in at Martinique, where the aircraft were put ashore and left to deteriorate in the open. Five other Model 77's found their way to the U.K., where the RAF gave them the name Cleveland, but they were not used operationally. Production of SBC-4's continued for the U.S. Navy, the overall total built of this version reaching one hundred and seventy-five by April 1940. In December 1941 the USN had a hundred and seventeen SBC-4's on strength; they equipped, *inter alia*, Marine Squadron VMO-151 and two USN squadrons in USS *Hornet* (VB-8 and VS-8), and were the last combat biplanes to be manufactured in the U.S.A.

21 Fairey III series

The successive models making up the Fairey III series of general-purpose/bomber aircraft rank second only to the variants of the Hawker Hart as the most extensively-built British military biplanes of 1919–39. In fact the design originated before the end of World War 1, the progenitor of the series being the Fairey III twin-float seaplane (N10) built to Admiralty requirements in 1917. This prototype was converted to landplane configuration to become the Fairey IIIA, fifty production examples of which were ordered for the RNAS/RAF. Comparatively few of these had been delivered by November 1918, and in 1919 those in service were withdrawn. Powerplant of the IIIA, the 260 hp Sunbeam Maori II, was retained in the Fairey IIIB, which introduced an increase of nearly 50 per cent in the span of the upper wings, from 46 ft 1¼ in (14·05 m) to 62 ft 9 in (19·13 m). Thirty twin-float Fairey IIIB's were ordered as naval bombers, but the final six aircraft on this contract were completed as Fairey IIIC's, as were those on a second production order for thirty IIIB's, with equal-span wings of the original dimension. The IIIC also introduced the 375 hp Rolls-Royce Eagle VIII engine. It was classified officially as a general-purpose aircraft, which in practice meant that it combined the scouting functions of the IIIA with the bomber responsibilities of the IIIB. The IIIC served until the autumn of 1921, and at about this time the first of six additional IIIC's (Fairey numbers F.328–333) were handed over to the (later Royal) Australian Air Service. Despite their short period with the RAF, some of the Fairey IIIC's were involved in active service in 1919, when a small number from HMS *Pegasus*, forming a part of the British North Russian Expeditionary Force, flew offensive sorties against the Bolshevik forces from their station at Archangel. In August 1920 the first example was flown of the Fairey IIID. This was destined to become the second most numerous model: two hundred and seven were built, of which fifty-six had the Eagle engine and the remainder a 450 hp Napier Lion. The IIID served predominantly with Fleet Air Arm units, in both landplane and seaplane versions, and was involved in the protection of British interests in the Shanghai area of China in 1927. More spec-

tacular fame was however achieved by four RAF machines (S1102–1105), which in March/April 1926 made the first official long-distance formation flight by RAF aircraft and its first from England to South Africa. They returned to Britain in the following June, having covered between them 13,900 miles (22,369 km) without even the slightest mechanical failure of any of the aircraft. The final and most numerous variant was the Fairey IIIF, of which the first of two prototypes (N198) was flown for the first time on 19 March 1926. The IIIF was of more elegant appearance, having a rounded-contour fin and rudder and a much neater installation of its Lion engine. After completion of an initial batch of ten IIIF's, a second series of forty was laid down, in the course of which a basic metal construction was adopted in place of the wood-and-metal structure used previously. Eventual production of the IIIF to Air Ministry contracts totalled five hundred and ninety-seven (including prototypes). Of these, over ninety are known to have been converted to, or completed as, Fairey Gordons; three were supplied to the Greek Air Force and one each to Egypt and New Zealand. There were numerous variations of the Fairey IIIF, inevitably in view of the quantity built, but the two main basic models were the 3-seat Mk III for naval units and the 2-seat Mk IV for the RAF. The IIIF first entered service with the RAF (No 47 Squadron) in 1927, and with the Fleet Air Arm (No 440 Flight) in 1928. The naval versions were not officially declared obsolete until January 1940, and three RAF machines were in service (then relegated to target-towing duties) more than a year after this.

22 Martin T3M/T4M

The design of these torpedo-bomber-scout biplanes was based upon a Curtiss torpedo-bomber, the CS-1, which first appeared in 1923. The Curtiss Aeroplane and Motor Co itself built only six CS-1's and two examples of the similar CS-2. Major production of the aircraft was undertaken by the Glenn L. Martin Company, which built thirty-five and forty respectively under designations SC-1 and SC-2. Martin then put to good use the experience gained in manufacturing these aeroplanes by offering an improved version to follow them into service in the second half of the 1920s. The major improvements included the introduction of a steel-tube fuselage, in which the front cockpit was sited further forward, and the use of the uprated T-3B version of the Wright Vee-type engine fitted in the SC-2. As before, a wheeled or twin-float landing gear could be utilised at the operator's option. No separate prototype was built of the T3M-1, as the new model was known. A Navy contract for twenty-four production aircraft was placed in October 1925, and delivery of these began in September of the following year. Like the SC-2, the T3M-1 had unequal-span wings, with the upper mainplane of shorter span than the lower. A change to

equal span, by extending the upper wing, was made in the next model, the T3M-2, which had individual cockpits in tandem for the three crew members and a change of powerplant to the 770 hp Vee-type Packard 3A-2500. One hundred T3M-2's were built, the first recipients of which were U.S. Navy Squadrons VT-1S and VT-2B, embarked in USS *Lexington* and *Langley*, in 1927. The first machine off the T3M-2 contract was retained by Martin for conversion as the XT3M-3 prototype (Hornet radial engine) and later the XT3M-4 (Wright Cyclone radial), but these did not go into production as such. The Navy did, however, order a new Hornet-engined prototype, the XT4M-1, which flew for the first time in April 1927 and featured reduced-span wings and a redesigned, horn-balanced rudder. Two production orders, totalling one hundred and two aircraft, were placed for the T4M-1, which began to enter service in August 1928 with VT-1B (*Lexington*) and VT-2B (*Saratoga*). In October of the same year Martin's Cleveland, Ohio, factory where the T4M's were manufactured was acquired by the Great Lakes Aircraft Corporation, and the latter company continued production of the type under TG-1 and TG-2 designations. These remained essentially similar to the T4M series except for the change from Hornet engines to Cyclones; the TG-1 (eighteen built) was powered by the R-1820-26 Cyclone and the TG-2 (thirty-two built) by the R-1820-86. These aircraft remained in U.S. Navy service until 1937.

23 Hawker Hart series

If Sydney Camm's elegant Fury represented the epitome of RAF biplane fighter design between the wars, there can be no doubt that his design of the Hart 2-seat day bomber, which spawned a host of other military variants, was one of the most technically and strategically significant bomber aircraft to emerge within the decade that followed the Armistice of November 1918. Together with its near-contemporary, the Fairey Fox, the Hart represented such a breakthrough in performance that it affected not only the future course of British light bomber development but that of fighter aircraft as well. It was Air Ministry Specification 12/26 that led Camm to seek the advantages of a powerful, low-drag, in-line engine to ensure the marked improvement in performance that was called for. Richard Fairey had found his answer in the United States, with the Curtiss D-12 engine; Camm, on the same track some three years later, based his design on a new Rolls-Royce engine, the Falcon. The use of an all-metal structure, the development of new methods of construction, and the period of development required for the powerplant, combined to delay the first flight of the prototype aircraft (J9052) until June 1928, and it did not appear in public until over a year later. By that time comparative trials against the Avro Antelope and Fairey Fox IIM had resulted in the issue of a production contract for the Hawker design. This was a modest order for fifteen Harts, delivery of which began in January 1930 to No 33 Squadron of the RAF at Eastchurch. Harts subsequently served with Nos 12, 15, 18, 21, 57 and 142 Squadrons in the U.K., with Nos 11, 39 and 60 in India and No 6 in Egypt and Palestine. The home-based aircraft began to be replaced by Hawker Hinds from late 1935, but those in India remained in service until 1939. Eventual British production of the Hart totalled nine hundred and eighty-four, approximately half of which were completed as Hart Trainers. Manufacture was shared between the parent company and Armstrong Whitworth (four hundred and fifty-six, mostly Trainers), Gloster (seventy-two) and Vickers (two hundred and twenty-six). Fifty-seven of the Hawker-built machines were designated Hart (India), a self-explanatory title indicating the provision of special equipment; another tropical-duty variant was known as the Hart (Special). The standard 2-seat bomber version was known as the Hart I or Hart SEDB (Single-Engined Day Bomber). The overall total given above includes six 2-seat fighters (later renamed Demon), and eight Harts exported to Estonia and four Pegasus radial-engined examples sold to Sweden in 1932 and 1934 respectively. In addition, a further twenty-four Pegasus-engined Harts were built at the Swedish State Aircraft Factory at Trollhättan in 1935–36. Many of these later fought with a Swedish volunteer squadron that served with the Finnish Air Force against the Soviet forces in the 'winter war' of 1939–40. Of the major Hart variants, the Hind bomber is dealt with elsewhere in this volume, and the Demon in the *Fighters 1919–39* volume; three others were the Audax, Hardy and Hector. The Audax, built for the Army Co-operation role, was identified by its long exhaust pipes and under-fuselage hook for message pick-ups. The general-purpose Hardy had a similar hook, plus underwing racks for supply containers, while the Hector (also an Army Co-operation type) was readily distinguishable by its changed nose contours, due to the installation of an 805 hp Napier Dagger H-type engine and the absence of sweepback on the upper wings. Six hundred and eighteen Audaxes were built (two hundred and forty-four by Avro, one hundred and forty-one by Bristol, twenty-five by Gloster, two hundred and sixty-five by Hawker and forty-three by Westland). Only forty-seven Hardys were completed, all of them by Gloster. One Hawker-built Hector prototype (modified from Hart K2434) was followed by one-hundred and seventy-eight production aircraft, manufactured by Westland. The Hart also had a naval counterpart in the Hawker Osprey, a fighter-reconnaissance version with deck-landing gear or a twin-float undercarriage. Prototype was a conversion of J9052, the original Hart, first flown in the new form in mid-1930. Hawker built one hundred and thirty-six, all for the Fleet Air Arm except one sold to Spain and four (with Pegasus radial engines) to Sweden; and eight others were built in Sweden. A developed version of the Audax, with Kestrel V engine, for South Africa was known as the Hartbees. Four Hawker-built Hartbees were supplied in 1935, after which sixty-five were built at Pretoria for the SAAF.

24 Douglas DT and World Cruiser

The first product of the Douglas Aircraft Co after its formation in 1920 was a single Liberty-engined civil biplane known as the Cloudster, and in some measure this contributed to the evolution of the first Douglas military aircraft, designed in 1921. This was the DT-1, a single-seat unstaggered biplane powered by a 400 hp Liberty engine, having an interchangeable landing gear of wheels or twin floats, and intended for the torpedo-bomber role. The U.S. Navy ordered three DT-1's for trials in 1921, but only one was actually delivered as a DT-1, distinguishable by having twin radiators mounted on the sides of the fuselage. The other two machines were completed as DT-2's, built as 2-seaters with single nose-mounted radiators but otherwise similar to the DT-1. A further sixty-four DT-2's were built, thirty-eight by Douglas, twenty by the LWF Engineering Co and six by the Naval Aircraft Factory. Delivery of these was made between 1922–24, initially to the San Diego

Naval Air Station and subsequently to other USN torpedo-bomber squadrons. The DT-2 could carry a single 1,835 lb (832 kg) torpedo beneath the forward fuselage, and had foldable wings to facilitate stowage on board ship. Some DT-2's were later redesignated following conversion to different powerplants. These included four of the NAF machines, which became DT-4's when fitted with Wright T-2 engines; two of them later had a geared T-2, with which they became DT-5's. The sole DT-6 was one of the Douglas-built DT-2's with a 450 hp Wright P-1 radial engine. Later in their career, which ended in 1926, some of the DT-2's were utilised as scout, observation or armament training aircraft; these included three of the LWF-built machines specially converted as SDW-1 long-range scouts with increased fuel tankage in an enlarged fuselage. By far the best-known aircraft of the DT type, however, were not Navy machines at all: they were four specially-modified aircraft ordered by the U.S. Army to participate in a six-nation competition to make a complete round-the-world flight in 1924. They were ordered after trials in the preceding year with a prototype aircraft (23–1210), and were basically similar to the Navy DT-2. They were stripped of non-essential military equipment, fitted with dual controls and RDF (Radio Direction Finding) and provided with increased fuel tankage for the global flight. Designated DWC (Douglas World Cruiser), the four aircraft

were delivered in March 1924. They were numbered 1 to 4 and named, respectively, *Seattle*, *Chicago*, *Boston* and *New Orleans*. Three of them left Clover Field, California, for Seattle on 17 March 1924, on the first leg of their journey, being joined there the following day by the fourth machine. All four left Seattle on 6 April, but soon lost *Seattle*, which crashed near Port Moller, Alaska, on 30 April. The remaining three had almost completed their global tour (during which no less than twenty-nine engines were used in the four aircraft) before *Boston* was forced to ditch in the North Atlantic on 3 August during the homeward flight. The two survivors were joined at Nova Scotia by the original prototype (now named *Boston II*), arriving safely back at Seattle on 28 September 1924 after a 175-day flight covering some 28,000 miles (45,062 km). The *Chicago* and *New Orleans* still survive as exhibits in the National Air Museum, Washington, and the USAF Museum at Wright-Patterson Air Force Base, Dayton, Ohio.

25 **Hawker Horsley and Dantorp**

A robust and efficient load-carrier, the Horsley day bomber/torpedo bomber survived early development troubles to serve with six RAF squadrons at home or overseas until 1935, twelve years after it had been designed. It was evolved to the requirements of Specification 26/23 (for a medium day bomber), and was selected in preference to three other contenders. The prototype (J7511) flew for the first time in 1925, powered by a Rolls-Royce Condor III engine, but during that year the load-carrying requirements were raised to a maximum of 1,500 lb (680 kg) of bombs or a 2,150 lb (975 kg) torpedo; it is to the Horsley's credit that these requirements could be met with comparatively little structural alteration. A second prototype (J7721) was followed by the production of an initial batch of twenty aircraft, delivery of which began in January 1927 to No 11 Squadron of the RAF at Netheravon. One hundred and twenty-eight production Horsleys were eventually built. Six of these were sold to the Greek Navy in 1929; the remainder served with Nos 11, 15, 33, 36, 100 and 504 Squadrons in the U.K. and Singapore. Although the Horsley had begun life as a wood-and-fabric aeroplane, all-metal construction of the airframe was introduced at an early stage, possibly during the initial production batch. The two versions were designated respectively Horsley I and Horsley II. One Horsley (J8607), flown by Flight Lieutenant C. R. Carr, briefly held the world long distance record for a flight of 3,420 miles (5,504 km) between Cranwell and the Persian Gulf on 20–22 May 1927; but Charles Lindbergh's transatlantic flight in the *Spirit of St Louis* ended in Paris later the same day, and surpassed the Horsley's performance. Standard powerplant of the Horsleys in service was the 665 hp Rolls-Royce Condor IIIA,

but several Horsleys were used as flying test-beds for over a dozen alternative engines. One of these, the 805 hp Armstrong Siddeley Leopard IIIA 14-cylinder radial, was installed in two Horsley-type aircraft delivered to the Danish Naval Air Service in 1932. The Danish government acquired a licence to manufacture this version, which became known as the Dantorp, at the Naval Dockyard at Copenhagen, but in the event none were built in Denmark. Nevertheless the two Hawker-built Dantorps (serials 201 and 202), which were 3-seaters, carried out a considerable amount of flying, remaining in use until destroyed by Danish patriots at Holmen naval base in 1940 to prevent them falling into German hands. Danish designation of these aircraft was H.B.III (Hydro-Biplane Type III).

26 Blackburn Shark
The name of the Blackburn Aircraft and Motor Co (later Blackburn Aircraft Co) between the two world wars was virtually synonymous with the provision of torpedo-bomber/reconnaissance aircraft for the Fleet Air Arm. From 1923 onward, Blackburn built between two hundred and twenty and two hundred and fifty examples of successive swept-wing biplane designs known as the Dart, Blackburn, Ripon and Baffin. The final biplane design, before the appearance of the Skua and Roc monoplanes, was the 2/3 seat Shark torpedo/spotter/reconnaissance type. The Shark originated as a private-venture

design to Specification S.15/33, known as the B-6 and first flown in May 1934. This prototype was acquired by the Air Ministry and allocated serial number K4295, an initial contract for sixteen Shark I production aircraft being awarded in August 1934. The first deliveries were made to No 820 Squadron (HMS *Courageous*) in May of the following year. Not all of Blackburn's earlier naval types could by any means be described as attractive, but the Shark represented a cleaner aerodynamic design, notwithstanding the angularity of its wing and horizontal tail surfaces. Detail improvements only were introduced on the Shark Mk II, for which K4295 also acted as the prototype, and the 700 hp Tiger VIc engine was retained. One hundred and twenty-six Shark II's were completed. A 745 hp Perseus XIII engine and a glazed and sectioned enclosure for the crew distinguished the Shark III, ninety-five of which were built in 1937. In all, the Shark served operationally only with Nos 810, 820 and 821 Squadrons of the FAA, and with Nos 753 and 754 Training Squadrons. Its first line service was relatively short, for it was replaced by the Fairey Swordfish in 1938, but from then until the outbreak of war it gave useful service as a training machine for naval observers and telegraphists. It operated mostly as a landplane, but an interchangeable twin-float landing gear could be fitted if required. Six floatplane Shark II's were built for the Portuguese Navy in 1936. In April 1937 two Sharks with 840 hp Bristol Pegasus IX engines were supplied to Canada, where the Canadian Boeing factory subsequently built twenty similar aircraft under licence.

27 Curtiss SOC Seagull

The versatile Seagull has received less attention among aircraft of the inter-war years than it deserves, perhaps due to the prosaic nature of the duties it was required to perform. Yet it was built in substantial numbers and carried out a decade of useful service, outlasting the aircraft designed to replace it and, at the end, never being replaced at all. The prototype (serial number 9413), first flown in April 1934, was conceived initially purely for the observation role, being designated XO3C-1. It was powered by a Pratt & Whitney Wasp radial engine, seated two occupants in tandem in open cockpits and had a landing gear comprising a single central amphibious float and two stabilising floats beneath the outer lower wing panels. In March 1935 it was reclassified as a scout observation type, receiving the new designation XSOC-1, and an initial contract for one hundred and thirty-five production SOC-1 Seagulls was placed by the U.S. Navy. Delivery began later that year, the first aircraft being assigned to the cruiser USS *Marblehead* in November. Forty more SOC-1's were ordered in May 1936; these were redesignated SOC-2 late in 1937, signifying a different-model Wasp engine and a wheels-only landing gear. The

SOC-3 had interchangeable wheel or (non-amphibious) float gear, but was otherwise similar to the SOC-2; eighty-three were built by Curtiss and forty-four (designated SON-1) by the Naval Aircraft Factory at Philadelphia. Production (totalling three hundred and six, including the original prototype) was completed by three floatplane Seagulls built for the U.S. Coast Guard. These were given SOC-4 designations in 1943 when they came under Navy jurisdiction. During their career the Curtiss Seagulls served aboard every aircraft carrier, battleship and cruiser in the U.S. Fleet, as well as a number of lesser vessels. They were flown, *inter alia*, by U.S. Navy Squadrons VO-1 to VO-5, VCS-7, VCS-9, VS-5B, VS-6B, and VS-9S to VS-12S; one was used as personal aircraft of the C-in-C, U.S. Fleet. Two hundred and seventy-nine Seagulls were still in service in mid-1940, and three years later twenty-seven U.S. cruisers were still equipped with these aircraft. During the war the addition of arrester gear brought the new designations SOC-2A and SOC-3A. The Seagull's intended replacement, the SO3C, proved a disappointing type, and when it was withdrawn early in 1944 the surviving Seagulls were returned to an operational status which they maintained until the war was over.

28 Vickers Vimy and Vernon

Design of the Vickers Vimy originated in 1917, and its development during World War 1 is described in the *Bombers 1914–19* volume in this series. In the first full year of peace, two Vimys achieved world-wide renown for remarkable long-distance performances. The first of these was the Vimy flown by Captain John Alcock and Lieutenant Arthur Whitten-Brown, which took off from St John's, Newfoundland, on 14 June 1919 to attempt the first non-stop crossing of the Atlantic Ocean by aeroplane. After a perilous journey in atrocious weather, it force-landed in Derrygimla bog at Clifden, in County Galway, Northern Ireland, on the following day; both occupants were unhurt and were subsequently knighted for their achievement. Five months later, on 12 November 1919, two brothers, Lieutenants Ross and Keith Smith, left Hounslow in the Vimy G-EAOU to try to become the first Australians to fly to Australia from England. After a twenty-eight-day journey that, to say the least, was eventful, they arrived at Darwin at the end of their 11,130 mile (17,912 km) journey on 10 December 1919. Their achievement, too, was acknowledged by the award of a knighthood apiece. In February 1920 two South African Air Force officers, Lieutenant Colonel Pierre van Ryneveld and Major C. J. Quintin Brand, reached Bulawayo in the second of two Vimys used in their attempt to gain Cape Town from England, but they had to complete their journey in a borrowed D.H.9. At home, the Eagle-engined Vimy began to enter RAF service in quantity. Approximately two hundred and thirty-two Vimys were built, most of them by Vickers but with contributions by Morgan and Co, Westland and the RAE. The first RAF bomber squadron fully to equip with Vimys was No 58 in Egypt, which did so in July 1919, and these bombers later served with Nos 7 and 9 Squadrons in the U.K. and Nos 45 and 216 in the Middle East. Those of No 216 Squadron flew some of the first Cairo–Baghdad air mail flights. From 1921–25 they began to be replaced by a later Vickers bomber, the Virginia, although No 502 Squadron in Northern Ireland retained its Vimys until 1929. Thereafter about eighty were refitted with Bristol Jupiter or Armstrong Siddeley Jaguar radial engines, in which form they gave several further useful years of service at RAF Flying Training Schools or as parachute trainers. A few were still in existence as late as 1938, when they were made target aircraft for trainee crews of Army searchlights. A civil version was evolved in 1919, known as the Vimy Commercial, which had a huge bulbous oval fuselage for passenger-carrying. From this, in turn, evolved a military bomber-transport, the Vernon, which featured prominently in these joint roles in the skirmishes in Iraq and Cyprus in the early 1920s. They too played an important role in the Cairo–Baghdad air mail services, doing much to establish the routes eastward later flown on a commercial basis by Imperial Airways. A total of sixty Vernons was built, including five converted from Vimys, twenty Mk I, twenty-five Mk II and ten

Mk III; they were used by Nos 45 and 70 Squadrons.

29   **de Havilland D.H.10 Amiens**
A wartime design, the Amiens had its origins in the earlier D.H.3, which was powered by two Beardmore engines and test-flown in July 1916. The War Office actually ordered fifty production D.H.3's, but cancelled the contract before the first machine had been completed. However, to a new day bomber specification of April 1917 the de Havilland team offered a slightly enlarged version of the previous design, powered by two Siddeley Puma pusher engines and known as the D.H.10. Four prototypes were ordered, the first of which (C8658) made its maiden flight on 4 March 1918. It was followed on 20 April by an Eagle-engined second aircraft, after which it was decided to install tractor, not pusher, engines in all subsequent machines. By July 1918 contracts had been placed for no less than twelve hundred and seventy-five D.H.10's, known as the Amiens Mk III and based upon the third prototype, which had been flown with two of the 400 hp American Liberty engines. Due to the serious shortfall in supplies of the Liberty, however, only eight D.H.10's had been delivered to the RAF by 31 October 1918. The initial batch of sixteen aircraft had also included the first example of a modified version, the D.H.10A (Amiens IIIa), which had the engines mounted directly on the lower mainplanes instead of midway between the

wings as hitherto. The great scarcity of Liberty engines led initially to the adoption of the Rolls-Royce Eagle VIII, the designations D.H.10B and D.H.10C presumably covering Eagle-engined counterparts of the two original Liberty-powered models. Inevitably, production contracts were drastically reduced after the Armistice, and the number of D.H.10-type aircraft actually completed cannot be determined with any certainty; there are, however, known serial number allocations for two hundred and twenty-three, excluding prototypes, and the Amiens is known to have served with No 120 Squadron in the U.K., No 216 in Egypt, and No 60 (formerly 97) in India. Among its peacetime duties were included the carriage of air mail, both in Europe and in India, and in the latter country it was called into action against local tribal uprisings during 1920–23. It was officially withdrawn from RAF service in 1923.

30 **Boulton Paul Overstrand**

In April 1928 a new twin-engined medium day bomber entered service with No 101 Squadron of the RAF at Bircham Newton, Norfolk, so closing a gap in the RAF's armoury of combat aircraft that had existed since the withdrawal of the war-vintage D.H.10 five years earlier. This aircraft was the Boulton and Paul Sidestrand, designed by J. D. North and descended from his earlier but less successful designs, the Bourges and the Bugle. The first of two Sidestrand prototypes (J7938) was first flown in 1926, having been

designed to meet the requirements of Air Ministry Specification 9/24. Instead of the Napier Lion engines originally planned, the aircraft was powered by two 425 hp Bristol Jupiter VI radials; it had an excellent single-engined performance and was remarkably agile and easy to handle considering its size. Only one squadron of Sidestrands was formed, and only twenty aircraft were built. The prototypes were designated Mk I, and were followed by nine Mk II (six of which were later converted to Mk III) and nine built from the outset as Mk III's. The Mk III was distinguished from the Mk II by having geared Jupiter VIIIF engines instead of ungeared Jupiter VI's. One Sidestrand III (J9186) underwent conversion with various other powerplants, and then, to meet Specification 29/33, had the nose section completely remodelled when the original nose, mounting an open gun ring, was replaced by a fully-enclosed, power-operated gun turret. With this modification it was known first as the Sidestrand V and then by the new name Overstrand, following an order in March 1934 to convert three additional Sidestrands to a similar standard. Other modifications were made to the fuselage and landing gear, and the 580 hp Bristol Pegasus IIM.3 engine was adopted as powerplant. Nineteen production Overstrands were ordered to Specification 23/34, and these were delivered as ready to No 101 Squadron as replacements for the Sidestrands. Five more Overstrands were built in

1935, and the type served with No 101 Squadron until replaced by Blenheim monoplane bombers in August 1938. Thereafter they were employed as bombing and gunnery trainers until mid-1940, when all surviving Overstrands were grounded. A projected development of 1935, known as the Superstrand, reached the stage of being re-engined with 720 hp Pegasus IV engines, but the retractable landing gear proposed for this aircraft was never fitted and further work on the project was abandoned.

31 **Martin MB-1 and MB-2**

During the year and a half of its involvement in World War 1, the United States relied almost entirely upon European aircraft industries for the provision of its combat aircraft. One of these types was the Handley Page O/400 bomber, which was also built under licence in the U.S., and it was to find a successor to the British type that Glenn Martin was asked by the U.S. government in 1917 to design a new bomber, with a performance superior to the Handley Page machine and a secondary capability as an aeroplane for both visual and photographic reconnaissance missions. Martin's answer was a twin-engined, twin-tailed biplane, powered by 400 hp Liberty engines and bearing the company designation MB-1. In January 1918 Martin was awarded a contract for ten of these new aircraft, and the first of them made its maiden flight on 17 August of the same year. This and the next three machines were

equipped for the observation role, while the fifth, sixth and seventh MB-1's were completed to bomber configuration, carrying a crew of four, a five-gun armament and a maximum bomb load of 1,040 lb (472 kg). The three final MB-1's on the initial contract were completed as experimental aircraft. The eighth had augmented fuel capacity, increasing the range from the normal 390 miles (628 km) to 1,500 miles (2,414 km); the ninth, a bomber, had a final installation of a 37 mm cannon on the nose; and the tenth was completed as a transport, seating ten passengers in a much-modified fuselage stripped of its military equipment. None of these modifications went into production, although a second MB-1 was later converted to the transport configuration. This aircraft was one of four additional MB-1's built for the U.S. Army; two others were built for evaluation as torpedo-bombers by the U.S. Navy (which then ordered ten as TM-1's), and six 'civilianised' MB-1's were completed for use by the Government Postal Service. In 1919–20 Martin evolved a developed version, known as the MB-2, for night bomber duties. Dimensionally, this was not much different from the MB-1, although it weighed about a ton more and was powered by uprated Liberty 12 engines of 420 hp in nacelles of modified shape, mounted directly on the lower wings and with overhead radiators instead of the frontal radiators of the MB-1 installation. In addition, whereas on the MB-1 all except the outermost bays of interplane struts were canted outward at an angle of about 60 degrees, those of the MB-2 were all of an upright nature. As on the MB-1, the wing panels of the MB-2 outboard of the engine nacelles could be folded back alongside the fuselage – a feature inherited from the Handley Page O/400. In 1920 Martin received an Army contract for five MB-2's and fifteen identical aircraft given the Army designation NBS-1 (Night Bomber, Short Range). A further fifty NBS-1's were ordered from Curtiss, thirty-five from the LWF Engineering Co, and twenty-five from Aeromarine. The MB-2/NBS-1 remained in service until 1927–28, when it was replaced by the Keystone LB types. It was an aircraft of this type which sank the former German battleship *Ostfriesland* during the demonstration of bombing techniques given to U.S. officials in July 1921 by Colonel 'Billy' Mitchell.

32 Keystone LB series

The rather complicated assortment of twin-engined LB (Light Bomber) types produced by the Keystone Aircraft Corporation in the middle 1920s actually derived from a single-engined biplane bomber. This was the LB-1, one prototype and nine service trials specimens of which were produced in 1923–26 by the Keystone Company under its former title of Huff-Daland and Co Inc. It was the basic airframe of the 3-seat LB-1 that was adapted to become the Keystone prototype XLB-3A. The single nose-mounted Packard engine was replaced by two 410 hp Pratt & Whitney Wasp radials, mounted midway between the upper and lower wings; accommodation was increased to five crew members, and the bombardier's station was located in the more traditional nose position instead of amidships as on the LB-1. First production bomber was the LB-5, ten of which were completed with 420 hp Liberty engines mounted on the lower wings and vertical tail surfaces consisting of a single central main rudder and two smaller rudders outboard. The later configuration was replaced, in the twenty-five LB-5A's which followed, by a more conventional arrangement of twin fins and rudders of equal size. The tapered wing planform, inherited from the LB-1, disappeared in the prototype and seventeen production LB-6's which followed, in favour of wings of constant chord throughout; and the Liberty engines were replaced by 525 hp Wright Cyclones mounted in the mid-gap position. Thus modified, this airframe became the standard configuration for the remainder of the LB series. Major production models were the LB-7 and LB-10A. Eighteen of the former and sixty-three of the latter were built, all with 525 hp Pratt & Whitney Hornet engines; the LB-10A was distinguished by having a single instead of a twin tail assembly. Single examples were completed, with various-model Cyclone or Hornet engines, of the LB-8, LB-9, LB-10, LB-11/11A and LB-12; and the Keystone LB range was completed by orders for seven

LB-13's and three LB-14's. However, in 1930 it was decided to discontinue the differentiation by designation of the U.S. Army's light and heavy bomber categories, and a new series of bomber designations was introduced using the single prefix letter B. Under this arrangement the LB-10A's became known (before they had actually been delivered) as B-3A's. The LB-13's became single-tailed Y1B-4's or Y1B-6's; the LB-14's were redesignated Y1B-5, though their completion or delivery has not been confirmed. The final twenty-seven LB-10A/B-3A machines later had Cyclone engines installed in place of their original Hornets, and in this form received yet another designation, B-5A. The final production models, built in 1932 after the designation confusion had settled down, were the B-4A (twenty-five built) and B-6A (thirty-nine built). These were both single-tailed models, powered respectively by Hornet and Cyclone engines, all of 575 hp.

33 Curtiss BT-32 Condor

In the spring of 1932 a Curtiss design team led by G. A. Page, Jr, began the detail design of a low-cost commercial biplane transport aircraft as an interim project to assist in the company's recovery from the economic depressions of the years immediately before. Prior to this Page had already projected an experimental transport design with the company designation XT-32, and it was decided to continue developing this to meet the new requirement. The T-32 Condor prototype flew for the first time on 30 January 1933, and was of conventional biplane layout with non-staggered wings and powered by two of the then-new Wright Cyclone radial engines in neatly-contoured nacelles mounted on the lower wings. In its detail design the Condor offered several novel features intended to make it attractive to potential customers, but its most readily noticeable attraction was the almost fully-retractable main landing gear, of which only the tips of the wheels protruded from the engine nacelles. Modest but welcome orders were received from two American airlines, and two of the original-type T-32 Condors were also acquired by the U.S. Army Air Corps and given the transport designation YC-30. The introduction in 1934 of supercharged Cyclone engines, driving variable-pitch propellers, brought a change in the company designation to AT-32, and from the twenty-second aircraft onward all Condors built as transports were of this basic type. Two of these were supplied to the U.S. Navy, which used them in service under the designation R4C-1; their final role was in 1940–41 with the U.S. expedition to the Antarctic, where they were then abandoned. (Another T-32, the twenty-first Condor built, also served in the Antarctic with the expedition led by Admiral Richard Byrd.) When the advent of the Boeing 247 and Douglas DC-2 all-metal monoplane airliners offered a clear challenge to the further sales of biplane airliners, Curtiss decided to adapt the Condor design to a bomber role, with a particular eye upon the foreign market among the world's smaller (or at any rate less wealthy) air forces. Here the Condor's load-carrying ability stood it in good stead, and in its modified BT-32 form it could accommodate up to 1,100 lb (499 kg) of bombs within the fuselage and a further seven 25 lb (11 kg) bombs beneath each lower wing. Work on the re-modelling to bomber configuration began during 1933, and a demonstration aircraft was flown for the first time in February 1934. The final Condor development, known as the CT-32, was evolved as a freight transport, and has a strong claim to be considered the first aircraft designed especially for this role. Out of an overall total of forty-five Condors built, fourteen went to military customers. These were the air forces of Colombia (three BT-32's), Nationalist China (two T-32's, four AT-32's and the BT-32 demonstrator) and Peru (one BT-32); and the Argentine Navy (three CT-32's).

34   Lioré et Olivier LeO 20

In June 1924 the first flight took place of a 2-seat, twin-engined bomber biplane designed by the Lioré et Olivier company and known as the LeO 12. Five prototypes, each powered by two 400 hp Lorraine engines, were built and later served with an experimental French squadron in the capacity of night bomber. A civil transport version of this design was built as the LeO 121, and in 1926 a new prototype appeared which had a powerplant of two Gnome-Rhône (Bristol) Jupiter radial engines. This aircraft, the LeO 122, did not itself go into production, but did act as prototype for a similar but slightly larger bomber, the LeO 20. The LeO 20 was a 4/5-seat night bomber, having a rather cumbersome appearance (and performance), with three-bay equal-span rectangular wings, a deep, capacious box-like fuselage and a non-retractable 'trousered' main undercarriage. Three hundred and twenty LeO 20's were built for the French Air Force, with whom the aircraft remained in service until 1937, despite its unspectacular performance. Several were utilised for experimental purposes, including one LeO 20 with much-reduced lower wing span and area, one mounting a 37 mm cannon on the nose and another with different-model Gnome-Rhône engines fitted with superchargers. A small number were later converted for use as paratroop trainers, and in this form were redesignated LeO 201. In addition to those supplied to the *Aéronautique Militaire*, two LeO 20's were supplied to Brazil and seven to Rumania. The basic design was taken a stage further after the LeO 202 (which had two Salmson 9 Abc engines) by making it into a four-engined aircraft; the first such model was the LeO 203, which flew for the first time in March 1931. This had four Gnome-Rhône engines mounted in tandem pairs on the lower mainplanes, each pair driving one tractor and one pusher propeller. A similar arrangement of four Renault 9 Ca engines was installed in the LeO 205 (the LeO 204 having been the prototype of a proposed naval version). Neither the LeO 203 nor the 205 entered production as such, but forty examples were built from 1932 of the LeO 206, based on the former prototype. Although powered with four supercharged 350 hp Gnome-Rhône 7 Kds engines, the LeO 206 differed from the 203 prototype in having a large ventral gondola incorporating a belly-gunner's position. Development of the series ended with three LeO 207's (Gnome-Rhône Titan-Major engines) and, in 1936, one LeO 208, a much-redesigned version with narrow-chord lower wings, uprated Gnome-Rhône 14-series engines and a retractable main landing gear. The latter offered a considerably better performance than the original LeO 20, but development was not pursued.

35 Vickers Virginia, Victoria and Valentia

The Virginia, which served with the RAF for fourteen of the years between the two world wars, was developed originally as a long-range bomber to supersede the Vimy. The design was based largely upon that of the Vimy, and the prototype Virginia I (J 6856), powered by two 450 hp Napier Lion engines, flew for the first time on 24 November 1922. Numerous modifications were introduced as flight testing progressed, one of them being the experimental addition of nacelles (known as 'fighting tops') to the

upper wings, each with emplacements for one gunner at the front and one at the rear. A second machine (J6857, Virginia II) flew in the spring of 1924, having a lengthened nose, improved engine installation and other refinements. Later that year the Virginia I made the first of several flights with Rolls-Royce Condor III engines, and subsequently, with a lengthened fuselage and redesigned nose, it became the solitary example completed of the Virginia Mk VIII. With the Lion engines reinstated, and sweepback applied to the outer panels of the wings, it represented a Mk VII, and eventually, late in 1928, was rebuilt to Mk X standard. The first production version of the Virginia was the Mk III, six of these being completed to Specification 1/21 with uprated Lion engines and delivered to No 7 Squadron in 1923. They were followed by three Mk IV (externally similar but with a bigger bomb load) and twenty-two Mk V (similar to the Mk III but with a third, central rudder). So far, production Virginias had had dihedral on the lower wings only, but the twenty-five Virginia VI bombers ordered in 1924–25 incorporated this feature on both mainplanes; six Mk V's were eventually modified in a similar way. Main features of the Mk VII were its sweptback outer wings, redesigned nose and a lengthened rear fuselage, all of which combined to make the Virginia easier to fly and a more efficient combat aeroplane. Only eleven new-production Mk VII's were built, but the improvements were such that thirty-eight earlier Virginias were converted to bring them up to Mk VII standard. One of the latter machines (J7131) became the prototype for the Virginia IX: this was the first model to introduce a tail gun position (considered preferable to the 'fighting tops' concept tried out earlier), whose extra weight was counteracted by a wider-span tail and lengthened nose. Most of the thirty-five Virginia IX's were conversions, only eight being built as new aircraft. The last Virginia, the Mk X, was also the version built in the greatest numbers, largely as a result of the improvements gained by changing to all-metal construction. Fifty new Mk X's were built, and a further fifty-three existing aircraft were rebuilt to similar standard. Total production of Virginia aircraft was only one hundred and twenty-six aircraft; yet from 1923, Virginias of various marks served with nine front-line RAF bomber squadrons in the U.K. (Nos 7, 9, 10, 51, 58, 214, 215, 500 and 502) until late in 1937, alongside such later designs as the Hinaidi and Heyford, and some were known to be still flying in 1941. A transport variant, bearing the same relationship to the Virginia as the Vernon had done to the Vimy, was known as the Victoria. The prototype (J6860) flew on 22 August 1922, and ninety-seven Victorias were built, serving with Nos 9, 48, 53, 58, 70 and 216 Squadrons. Production versions were designated Mks III to VI; like the Vernons, they gave most of their service in the Middle East and India. A Pegasus-engined development was known as the Valentia; twenty-eight of these were built, and a further fifty-four produced by converting former Victorias.

36 Handley Page Hyderabad and Hinaidi

Both the Hyderabad and the Hinaidi were produced for the RAF to fulfil the role of a 4-seat heavy night bomber, although only two RAF squadrons (and two of the Auxiliary Air Force) were ever equipped with them. The Hyderabad was evolved from Handley Page's W 8b commercial airliner, and was at first known as the W 8d or H.P. 24. The prototype, developed to meet Air Ministry Specification 31/22, was in its original form little different from the W 8b, apart from the airframe strengthening necessary to transport the required bomb load. It bore the serial number J6994, and flew for the first time in October 1923. Construction was mainly of wood, with fabric-covered wings, fuselage and tail unit, and a four-wheel main landing gear was fitted. After the first flight J6994 was fitted with a redesigned, more angular fin and rudder, which became standard on subsequent aircraft of the type. An initial production batch of fourteen Hyderabads was ordered, to Specification 15/24, and the first deliveries were made to No 99 Squadron at Bircham Newton in December 1925. The second Hyderabad squadron was No 10 at Upper Heyford, which did not begin re-equipping with these bombers until January 1928. Three additional contracts were placed which brought the total number of Hyderabads ordered (including the prototype) to forty-five; but not all were completed as such, for they were withdrawn from first-line service in 1930 in favour of a new version of the design. This was the H.P. 33 Hinaidi, the prototype of which was converted from an early production Hyderabad (J7745) and first flown in its new guise on 26 March 1927. The Hyderabad had been powered by two 450 hp Napier Lion engines; in the Hinaidi I these were replaced by a pair of 440 hp Bristol Jupiter VIII radials driving propellers of increased diameter. Construction, as before, was of wood with fabric covering. Seven new Hinaidi I's were built, in addition to which the last six Hyderabads were completed to the same standard and at least two earlier Hyderabads were converted. Then, on 25 November 1931, the prototype H.P. 36 Hinaidi II (J9478) was flown for the first time. Although retaining the fabric-covered general appearance of its predecessors, the Hinaidi II's airframe was of metal construction, and this version could also be distinguished by the moderate sweepback of the upper and lower wings outboard of the engine centre-lines. Thirty-three production Hinaidi II's were built, to Specification 13/29, and these began to join the Mk I's in service with Nos 10 and 99 Squadrons from 1932. They were replaced by Heyfords from late 1933, serving for a few years thereafter (as the Hyderabads also had done) with Nos 502 and 503 Squadrons of the AAF. The first production Hinaidi I (J9030) was completed for trials in a troop-carrying role, and presumably in support of this proposal Handley Page also produced a transport version of its two bombers in response to Specification C.20/27. This was the H.P. 35, known originally as the Chitral and later as the Clive. The first Clive I (J9126) was something of a hybrid, having the wood-and-fabric airframe of the Hyderabad and the Jupiter engines and sweptback wings of the Hinaidi II. It could carry 17 troops or 10 stretchers, and could also be utilised as a bomber if required. However, only two further machines were built, these having metal airframes and being designated Clive II. They saw service with the RAF's Heavy Transport Flight at Lahore, in India; the Clive I was transferred to the civil register in August 1932.

37 Handley Page Heyford

No 99 Squadron, at Upper Heyford, was appropriately the first RAF unit to be equipped with the Heyford 4-seat night bomber, which it began to receive in December 1933. The bomber had been designed to Specification B.19/27, issued six years earlier, for a new type to replace both the Hinaidi and the Vickers Virginia. Two designs were accepted, the other being the Fairey Hendon monoplane, which was built in smaller numbers and did not enter service until late 1936. The H.P. 38 Heyford prototype

(J9130) was designed under Mr G. R. Volkert of Handley Page, and made its first flight at the company's newly-acquired airfield at Radlett, Hertfordshire, in June 1930. The Heyford's configuration was, for a biplane, unorthodox in the extreme, but this very unorthodoxy no doubt had a strong influence upon its selection. The upper wing was shoulder-mounted on the fuselage and bore the installation of the two Rolls-Royce Kestrel II engines. Heavy interplane struts then supported the lower mainplane at some considerable distance beneath the fuselage, and below this wing were the very substantial main landing wheels, protected by large fairings attached to the wing's leading-edge. This layout gave the Heyford a height on the ground of 20 ft 6 in (6·25 m), allowing fitters and ground crew head-high clearance to walk beneath the front fuselage and permitting servicing to be carried out very quickly indeed. From an operational standpoint the fields of view and fire enjoyed by the gunners and other crew members were exceptionally good, though care was obviously more than usually necessary when landing the aircraft. The first production model was the H.P. 50 Heyford I, with open cockpit and Kestrel IIIS engines, and the similar Mk IA with a motor-driven instead of wind-driven generator. Thirty-eight Mk I/IA's were built to Specification B.23/32, one Mk I (K 3503) being completed with an enclosed crew cabin. The open cockpit was retained on the sixteen Kestrel VI-powered

Heyford II's which followed in 1934. The engines in these aircraft were derated, but in the seventy Heyford III's which completed the bomber's production they were allowed to develop their full 640 hp each. In all, the Heyford served with eleven first-line RAF bomber squadrons in the U.K.: Nos 7, 9, 10, 38, 78, 97, 99, 102, 148, 149 and 166. From 1937, with the advent of first Whitley and then Wellington monoplane bombers, it began to be withdrawn from these units, but continued to serve in a training capacity until the early part of World War 2.

38 Kawasaki Ki-32

After ten years as Kawasaki's chief designer, Dr Richard Vogt returned to his native Germany in 1933, leaving the way clear for the emergence of individual Japanese designers within the company. One of these was Dr Takeo Doi, who had developed Vogt's Army Type 92 fighter into its ultimate version, the Ki-10. Another was Dr Isamu Imachi, from whom stemmed a neat low/mid-wing design for a 2-seat light bomber monoplane in 1936. After the completion of a wooden mock-up of this aeroplane in the summer of 1936, the first of eight prototypes was flown for the first time in March 1937. Powerplant for these prototypes – at a time when most Japanese designers still favoured radial engines – was the Ha-9-IIB Vee-type engine, the cooling system of which gave some trouble until a glycol system was introduced in place of the original water cooling. Apart from this, service tests proved satisfactory, and in July 1938 the aircraft entered service as the Ki-32 or Army Type 98 light bomber. It saw extensive service with the JAAF during the 1938–39 campaigns against China, particularly in the Hangkow and Wuchang operational theatres, and its duties included ground attack and reconnaissance in addition to light bombing. Despite liability to suffer from engine crankshaft failures, the Ki-32 was still in service at the outbreak of the Pacific war, although little was seen of it in front-line operations after the fall of Hong Kong. It was allocated the Allied code name 'Mary'. Production ended in the spring of 1940, by which time Kawasaki had completed eight hundred and forty-six Ki-32's in addition to the eight prototypes.

39 **Northrop A-17 and 8A series**
During the second half of 1933 the Northrop Corporation produced as a private venture an attack bomber, the Model 2C, based upon its successful Gamma and Delta commercial monoplanes and powered by a 712 hp Wright Cyclone radial engine. This prototype was acquired in 1934 for evaluation by the USAAC, which gave it the designation YA-13, and at the end of the year placed an order for one hundred and ten bombers which were basically similar except in having Pratt & Whitney engines. Originally the 800 hp Wasp was specified, but the aircraft (which were designated A-17) were actually built with 750 hp Wasp Juniors. The production A-17 also introduced a number of other modifications compared with the original prototype. The fully 'trousered' main wheel coverings were replaced by fairings which shrouded only the inner faces of the wheels; the wings were fitted with perforated flaps; and a proportion of the bomb load was carried internally. In 1936 these aircraft began to be joined in service by the first of one hundred and twenty-nine A-17A's, which had 825 hp Twin Wasp Junior engines and a retractable main undercarriage. Ninety-three of the latter were released for export in 1940, sixty-one of which were supplied to the RAF and the remainder to France. The French machines had only reached Martinique before the fall of France, and thus took no active part in the war, while most of the RAF machines (which were named Nomad) were transferred to the South African Air Force and employed on target-towing duties. Previous versions specifically for export appeared as early as 1935, when Northrop built for the Chinese Air Force about a hundred and fifty examples similar to its Model 2E prototype, which had a 750 hp Cyclone engine and two wing guns instead of four. Another prototype, the Northrop 8A-1, was bought by Sweden in 1937. This was fitted with a Bristol Mercury XXIV engine, and led to the licence manufacture in Sweden of one hundred and three aircraft, with designations B 5 to B 51). Thirty Northrop 8A-2's (840 hp Cyclone) were sold to the

Argentine Air Force. In August 1937 the Northrop company was acquired by the Douglas Aircraft Co, which continued to market the export versions as the DB-8A. Sales of these, with varying models of Cyclone engine, included ten DB-8A-3P's for Peru (1,000 hp), eighteen DB-8A-3N's to the Netherlands (1,050 hp), fifteen DB-8A-4's to Iraq (1,000 hp) and thirty-six DB-8A-5's (1,200 hp) to Norway. The invasion of Norway in 1940 forestalled delivery of the DB-8A-5's, which were instead diverted to Canada and flown in a training capacity by crews of Norwegian escapees. Thirty-one similar aircraft (of a Peruvian order for thirty-four) were commandeered by the USAAF in 1942. They were given the attack designation A-33, but, like the Norwegian machines, were also used mainly as training aircraft.

40   Douglas TBD Devastator

Two prototype designs were ordered by the U.S. Navy in mid-1934 as the first step towards securing a new generation of single-engined torpedo-bombers to serve in the newly-commissioned aircraft carrier USS *Ranger* and others of her class. One of these prototypes, the Great Lakes XTBG-1 biplane, was rejected on the grounds of instability and inadequate performance. The other contender, the Douglas XTBD-1, was an extremely clean-looking all-metal monoplane with an 800 hp XR-1830-60 (Pratt & Whitney Twin Wasp) engine and a retractable main undercarriage. This prototype (9720) flew for the first time on 15 April 1935 and continued to be test-flown for the next two years, gaining experience which was incorporated into the production model. The first production contract was placed in February 1936, and covered the manufacture of one hundred and fourteen TBD-1 Devastators, which thus became the first carrier-based monoplanes to be produced in quantity for the U.S. Navy. The first production Devastator was flown on 25 June 1937, and deliveries began in the following November. The first U.S. Navy Squadron to receive the new aircraft was VT-3, attached to the USS *Saratoga*, and by the time of America's entry into World War 2 Devastators had also been delivered to VT-2 (USS *Lexington*), VT-5 (*Yorktown*), VT-6 (*Enterprise*), VT-8 (shore-based at Norfolk, Virginia), VS-42 (*Ranger*) and VS-71 (*Wasp*). A second batch of TBD-1's ordered in August 1938 brought the overall production total to one hundred and twenty-nine. In 1939 the first production Devastator was fitted with twin Edo floats by the Naval Aircraft Factory. This aircraft was redesignated TBD-1A and used for a variety of test purposes over the next four years, but no series production of this version was undertaken. At the time of the attack on Pearl Harbor the U.S. Navy had a hundred Devastators on strength, of which sixty-nine were in first-line operational service. During the first six months of the war in the Pacific they were flown intensively against Japanese shipping or land targets, establishing a fine record of operational successes that reached their peak in the Coral Sea campaign of May 1942. But a month later, in the Battle of Midway Island, the remaining Devastators were decimated by the heavier and superior Japanese opposition, and thereafter those few which survived were withdrawn to serve out their time in various instructional capacities.

41 Loire-Nieuport LN-40 series

The LN-40 was the fourth basic design to be developed by the Société Anonyme Loire-Nieuport, following its formation in 1934 from the former Société Nieuport-Astra at Issy-les-Moulineaux and the Ateliers et Chantiers de la Loire. It was a single-seat dive-bomber, intended for employment by the one *Aéronautique Navale* in France's one and only aircraft carrier, the *Béarn*, and was designed by M Pillon of the former Nieuport company. The LN-40 clearly owed much to two of Pillon's earlier designs, the Ni 140 2-seat shipboard fighter and the Ni 161 single-seat land-based fighter, which had flown in prototype form in 1934–35 but which had not entered production. Construction of the LN-40-01 prototype (FW-0117) began in 1937, and this aircraft flew for the first time in June 1938. Like its near-contemporary, the Junkers Ju 87, the French dive-bomber had an inverted gull wing configuration, but was otherwise a much better-looking design, with a retractable main landing gear and a neatly-cowled 690 hp Hispano-Suiza 12

Xcrs Vee-type engine. To augment the vertical tail area, endplate fins were fitted to the tailplane before service trials began in September 1938; the lower portion of the central rudder was split vertically, dividing to right and left to serve the additional purpose of a dive brake. Six other LN-40's were ordered in 1936, before the prototype had flown, and after the first true production order was placed in February 1939 these also were completed to the same standard. This initial production model was designated LN-401, and began to be delivered to *Aéronavale* squadrons in the summer of 1939. By then the *Armée de l'Air* had also shown a belated interest in dive-bomber aircraft, and decided to order a land-based equivalent known as the LN-411. In the event, however, the performance of this model was found to be less than that which the *Armée de l'Air* required, and all but one of the forty LN-411's it had ordered were delivered instead to the French Navy. The fortieth machine was retained by the French Air Ministry and was later converted to become the prototype (and only example built) of the LN-42. The LN-401's and LN-411's did not enter squadron service (with *Escadrilles* AB-2 and AB-4) until after the outbreak of World War 2, by which time the *Béarn* was fully occupied in ferrying American combat aircraft from the U.S. to France. Consequently their operational careers took place from naval shore bases. Comparatively few of those completed pre-war survived after the fall of France in 1940, but a year later the occupying German authorities sanctioned the assembly for the Vichy Air Force of twenty-four LN-401/411 aircraft. These were completed, from recovered components, by the Châteauroux factory of the SNCA de l'Ouest (one of the new nationalised French companies, which had absorbed the former Loire-Nieuport concern in 1936). The LN-42 referred to above was a modified version, utilising the basic LN-401/411 fuselage together with a 1,100 hp HS 12Y-51 engine and wings of entirely new design. This was completed during the war years but, so far as is known, had made no proper flights before it was hidden to prevent confiscation by the German forces. It was eventually flown after the war, on 24 August 1945, but was by then too obsolescent a design to justify further development.

42　Heinkel He 70/170

The highly advanced aerodynamic and structural design exhibited by the He 70 would compare favourably enough even with some aircraft of the present day; that it should have been designed and built in little over six months, and flown at as early a date as 1932, is remarkable indeed. It was on 1 December of that year that the He 70V1 prototype, whose design had been inspired by Siegfried and Walter Günter, was flown for the first time, and during the early months of 1933 this aircraft and the first pre-production He 70A machine had set up a series of impressive new closed-circuit speed and speed-with-payload records which earned the aircraft the name *Blitz* (Lightning) from Deutsche Lufthansa, for whose use it had been designed. These early He 70's were powered by 630 hp BMW VI Vee-type engines, successive variants of which became the standard powerplant for the commercial He 70B, C, D and G models, of which a total of twenty-eight were built. In 1933 the He 70E model was evolved for light attack duties with the *Luftwaffe*, being based on the 750 hp He 70D and having underwing racks for small HE or incendiary bombs. Only a single rearward-firing MG 15 machine-gun was provided for defence, the aircraft relying upon its speed to escape attack. Its performance also made the He 70 potentially a most useful reconnaissance aircraft, and this requirement resulted in the appearance of the He 70F-0 and F-1 in 1934–35. Over long ranges, however, the twin-engined Dornier Do 17 proved a more practical choice, with the result that the He 70F was reallocated to a short-range communications role after a comparatively short period of first-line *Luftwaffe* service. During this time some eighteen He 70F's performed active reconnaissance and bombing duty with Germany's Condor Legion taking part in the Spanish Civil War of 1936–39. Seven were lost during that war but the survivors continued to serve for many years afterwards, the last not disappearing until the early 1950s. The He 170 was an export version, about twenty of which were completed in 1937–38 for the Hungarian Air Force. These differed from the standard He 70 in having 910 hp Gnome-Rhône 14K radial engines in place of the Vee-type BMW VI, and remained in Hungarian service until mid-1941. A prototype was flown in 1938 of the He 270, with a 1,175 hp DB 601A engine, but this version did not enter production.

43 Vickers Wellesley

By any standards, the Wellesley was a remarkable aeroplane. Most aircraft designers did not, at least in the early 1930s, normally think of long-range bombers in terms of elegant single-engined monoplanes with enclosed cockpits, cantilever wings and fully-retractable landing gear. But two men, at least, did – Barnes Wallis and Rex Pierson, whose ideas stemmed from the constructional methods used by Vickers to build the airship R.100. They applied these to a single-engined biplane, designed to Specification M.1/30, which flew in 1933, and Wallis developed it further in the aircraft selected by the Air Ministry as Vickers' contender to Specification G. 4/31, for a new RAF general-purpose and torpedo bomber. This G.4/31 machine was a rather ugly, bent-winged biplane, and was test-flown in 1934–35. Simultaneously, however, Vickers had proceeded with a private-venture contender to the same specification, with a more fully-developed geodetic structure and long-span cantilever monoplane wings. This flew for the first time on 19 June 1935, by which time the Air Ministry had already decided to order a hundred and fifty of the biplane bomber. But the disparity in performance between the two aircraft could not be ignored, and in the following September a new order superseded the earlier contract, calling for ninety-six of the G.4/31 monoplanes, which were given the type name Wellesley. The prototype was given the serial number K 7556 following numerous modifications, which included changing the Pegasus IIM.3 engine for a Pegasus X, increasing the rudder area and adding streamlined underwing containers to carry the bomb load. Geodetic construction was used for the thick-section high-aspect ratio wings, and for the fuselage aft of the wing front spar. Production Wellesley I's began to come off the assembly line early in 1937, and in April of that year No 76 Squadron at Finningley became the first RAF unit to equip with the new bombers; other squadrons to follow included Nos 35, 77, 148 and 207 in the U.K. and Nos 14, 45 and 223 in the Middle East. The home-based Wellesley formations were re-equipped with twin-engined types in 1939, but in Africa the Wellesley continued to serve in the early part of the war. A total of one hundred and seventy-six production Wellesleys were built. Of these, some of the later aircraft had a continuous 'glass-house' canopy bridging the front and rear cockpits, often being referred to (unofficially) in this form as Wellesley Mk II. In 1938 five aircraft

(L2637, '38, '39, '80 and '81) were specially converted for the RAF's Long Range Development Unit. They were powered by special Pegasus XXII engines, were stripped of their military equipment, and adapted to carry 1,290 Imp gallons (5,864 litres) of fuel instead of the normal maximum of 425 Imp gallons (1,932 litres). In July 1938, four of these aircraft made a 4,300-mile (6,920-km) non-stop flight from Cranwell to Ismailia via the Persian Gulf, in preparation for an attack on the world record for the greatest distance flown in a straight line. The attempt was made by three Wellesleys (L2638, L2639 and L2680), which took off from Ismailia on 5 November 1938 to reach Australia. The second aircraft was obliged to land at Timor to refuel, but the other two continued flying, through appalling weather, to land at Darwin nearly 48 hours after leaving Egypt.

44 Amiot 143

One of the major types of bomber equipping squadrons of the *Armée de l'Air* upon the outbreak of World War 2, the Amiot 143 resulted from a French Army requirement first issued in 1928. Four manufacturers submitted designs to meet this specification for a *Multiplace de Combat* day and night bomber, Amiot's proposal being the Type 140M which flew for the first time in 1931. Forty Amiot 140M's were ordered in 1933, but were never built as such because in the same year the requirement was changed to a multi-mission BCR

(*Bombardement, Chasse et Reconnaissance*) aircraft. Amiot built two new prototypes designated Type 143-01, to the revised specification, these aircraft being powered by two 740 hp supercharged Gnome-Rhône 14K radial engines; the first of these made its maiden flight in 1934. The new design was accepted for service, with modifications which included strengthening the fuselage, increasing the vertical tail area and fitting new gun turrets, and the forty aircraft ordered originally as Amiot 140M's were instead completed as 143M's. The first of these, which had 870 hp engines, was flown in April 1935, and deliveries began in the following July to GB III/22 at Chartres. Successive orders increased the number of Amiot 143's built by late 1938 to one hundred and seventy-eight. This total included one aircraft completed originally with 860 hp Hispano-Suiza 12 Ybrs Vee-type engines as the Amiot 142-01 prototype and later converted to 143 standard; and twenty-five ordered originally as Amiot 144's but completed instead as 5-seat day or 4-seat night bombers. The Amiot 143 served prior to the outbreak of World War 2 with many French bomber groups, including GB I/14, I/34, II/34, II/35, I/38, II/38 and II/63. Six bomber groups were equipped with these aircraft at the outbreak of war, and four were still so equipped in May 1940, when instead of their former leaflet raids over Germany they began to drop a more lethal cargo upon the enemy. They ended their days later in the war in the role of supply transport.

45 **Bloch 200**

The specification to which the Marcel Bloch 200 bomber was developed was issued in 1932, and resulted in the submission of eight different designs from six French manufacturers, among them the Farman 220 and 221. The objective was to find a suitable successor to the LeO 20 day and night bomber then in service with most French squadrons. Three prototypes of the Bloch design were ordered, and the first of these made its maiden flight in June 1933 powered by two 760 hp Gnome-Rhône 14 Krsd radial engines. In the following December an initial quantity of thirty production MB 200's was ordered, these aircraft being powered by Gnome-Rhône 14 Kirs/Kjrs engines. By agreement, only four of these machines (E-040 to E-043) were built by the Bloch works at Courbevoie, the remaining twenty-six (E-013 to E-038) being manufactured by the Potez factory at Méaulte. The first production Bloch 200 was flown in July 1934, and by the end of that year twenty had been delivered to the *Armée de l'Air*. With the placing of subsequent production orders the Société Hanriot at Bourges joined the manufacturing programme, which was stepped up to the extent that twelve *Escadres de Bombardement* were equipped with MB 200's by the end of 1935. The first squadrons to receive the type were I/12 and II/12 at Reims and II/22 at Chartres.

In mid-1935 a single MB 200 was supplied to Czechoslovakia, where one hundred and twenty-four aircraft of this type were subsequently built under licence by the Aero company, with Avia as sub-contractor. These differed from their French counterparts in having Walter-built Gnome-Rhône engines, fitted with NACA-type cowlings instead of Townend rings. Overall French production of the Bloch 200, excluding prototypes, amounted to two hundred and eight aircraft; these were built by Bloch (four), Breguet (nineteen), Hanriot (forty-five), Loire (nineteen), Potez (one hundred and eleven) and SA du Sud-Ouest (ten). The Sud-Ouest machines were intended for the *Aéronautique Maritime*, the remainder for the *Armée de l'Air*. Ninety-two were still in service at the outbreak of World War 2, but did not remain operational for long afterwards. By contrast, one hundred and fifty-five examples (out of a total of two hundred and fifty-three built for French use) were in service of the Bloch 210, a developed version of the MB 200 which had first flown in prototype form in November 1934. This had a redesigned fuselage and tail unit, but differed principally from its predecessor in having a low-wing configuration and the main landing gear fully-retractable into the nacelles of its 870 hp Gnome-Rhône engines. Thirty-five MB 210's were also produced for the Spanish Republican Air Arm, and a further ten for the Rumanian Air Force.

46 Potez 540 series

One of the new combat aircraft ordered under the French Air Ministry's Plan I was a new multi-seat design intended for service in the BCR (*Bombardement, Chasse et Reconnaissance*) category. Prior to the official adoption of Plan I in June 1934 General Denain (later appointed as France's Air Minister) had had private discussions with M Henry Potez at which the latter had agreed to produce, without formal contract, a prototype aircraft to meet this requirement. The resulting design was known as the Potez 540, and flew for the first time on 14 November 1933, less than three months after work on the design had begun. In its prototype form it had twin fins and rudders and was powered by two 690 hp Hispano-Suiza 12 Xbrs engines. Official acceptance trials were completed early in May 1934, by which time four pre-series examples of the Potez 540 had been ordered. The major changes from the prototype involved the substitution of a single fin and rudder and the adoption of HS 12 Xirs/Xjrs engines as the powerplant. Production began in 1934, the first series-built Potez 540M4 (multiplace, 4-seat) being delivered to the *Armée de l'Air* on 25 November of that year. The initial contract for thirty-nine aircraft was followed by others which raised the total output of the standard model (excluding the prototype and pre-series machines) to one hundred and eighty-five. In addition, three examples were built by the SNCAN factory at Méaulte of the Potez 540TOE, a version equipped for French colonial territories. One prototype was completed of the 5-seat Potez 541, which differed principally in having a powerplant of two 860 hp Gnome-Rhône 14 Kdrs radial engines. This was not adopted by the *Armée de l'Air*, but ten similarly-powered aircraft, designated Potez 543, were delivered to Rumania between 1936 and 1939. A further quantity was supplied to the Spanish Republican air force during the Civil War. The other major French model, also a 5-seater, was the Potez 542. Fifty-one (including a prototype) were built as Potez 542M5's, and sixteen others by SNCAN as Potez 542TOE's. They were powered by Lorraine Petrel Hdrs/Hers or Hfrs/Hgrs engines of 720 hp. The Potez 540/542 series served with a large number of French *Groupes de Reconnaissance*, reaching their peak of service in 1937. By the outbreak of World War 2 most of those still on strength were employed at French overseas bases in North Africa, the Middle East and Indochina, or at training establishments in France. One example was completed (possibly by conversion of an existing 540 or 542 airframe) as a Potez 544, powered by 860 hp HS 12 Ybrs engines and used as a liaison aircraft.

47 Martin B-10 series

A smooth, sleek monoplane with fully-enclosed bomb load and a retractable main undercarriage, the Martin B-10 was yet another classic example of what a good aircraft designer can do when not subservient to the limitations of an official specification. As the Martin Model 123, this twin-engined bomber design appeared in the early months of 1932, and the prototype was handed over to the U.S. Army in March of that year for evaluation with the designation XB-907. In its original form it had a top speed of 197 mph (317 km/hr), and when later modified as the XB-907A, with increased wing span, higher-powered Cyclone engines in long-chord cowlings and a rotatable gun turret in the nose, it added another 10 mph (16 km/hr) to this already-impressive figure. Such a performance clearly could not be ignored, and the award to Martin of the 1933 Collier Trophy was backed at the start of that year by a USAAC contract for forty-eight production examples of the new bomber. The first fourteen of these were completed as Cyclone-engined YB-10's for service trials, followed by one YB-10A with turbo-supercharged Cyclones, seven YB-12's with 775 hp Pratt & Whitney Hornet radials, one XB-14 with 950 hp Twin Wasp engines and twenty-five B-12A's, similar to the YB-12 but with increased fuel capacity. The manufacturer's designation for the production version was Model 139. First deliveries to the Army Air Corps were made in mid-1934, for the commencement of service trials, and in 1935 the aircraft began to reach operational units, among them the 2nd, 7th, 9th and 19th Bombardment Groups in the U.S. and other units in Panama and

Hawaii. Some Martins were converted to a twin-float landing gear and employed as coastal defence aircraft. Production and deliveries continued during 1935–36 with a further one hundred and three B-10B's, these reverting to the 775 hp Cyclone powerplant and incorporating detail improvements. Advanced though the Martin bomber was at the time of its first appearance, its first-line service in its intended role was relatively short, for it was overtaken in the late 1930s by the twin-engined Douglas B-18 and the four-engined long-range Boeing B-17. Consequently, in 1936 the U.S. government authorised the release of the Martin 139 design for export, and in this sphere the bomber achieved a commercial success equivalent to its production for the U.S. Army. The basic export version was known as the Model 139W, and was sold to Argentina (twenty-five), China (nine), the Netherlands Indies (one hundred and seventeen), Siam (six), Turkey (twenty) and the U.S.S.R. (one). Only the first thirty-nine of the Dutch East Indies Martins were Model 139W's, corresponding broadly to the B-10B; the remainder, designated Model 166, differed in having one long 'greenhouse' canopy embracing both the forward and rear cockpits.

48 Heinkel He 111
Altogether, the Heinkel He 111 was in service in one form or another somewhere in the world for some thirty years following its first appearance in the early months of

1937. The origin of its design actually dates from 1934, when the brothers Siegfried and Walter Günter first began to evolve it as an all-metal twin-engined monoplane of unusually clean lines. The He 111V1 prototype first flew on 24 February 1935, powered by a pair of 660 hp BMW VI inverted-Vee engines and equipped for a medium bomber role with three defensive 7·9 mm machine-guns and an internal bomb load of 2,205 lb (1,000 kg). Three other prototypes were completed; of these, the V2 and V4 were completed as 10-seat commercial passenger and mail transports. Some efforts were made to interest Deutsche Lufthansa in purchasing the aircraft, and the German airline did, later, operate six He 111C's and four He 111G's. The He 111V3 meanwhile served as the prototype for the first military pre-production version, the He 111A-0. Manufacture of this version began in mid-1935, and by the following spring aircraft of this model were being delivered for service trials to the *Luftwaffe* test centre at Rechlin. The He 111 was found to possess good handling qualities, and its handsome lines were clearly inherited from its single-engined predecessor, the He 70. It was, however, somewhat underpowered with the BMW engines, and for this reason the early-production He 111A-1's with these engines were rejected for squadron service.

The ten He 111 A-0's were sold to China. Production, therefore, continued with the He 111B-0 and B-1, in which two DB 600A engines were adopted as the powerplant. These in turn were followed by improved models, the He 111B-2 (DB 600C) and the He 111D-1 (DB 600G). In 1937 the He 111B-2 was among several modern German aircraft to participate in the Spanish Civil War, where it was one of the types flown regularly by Germany's Condor Legion. In Spain, the He 111's performance was such that it could outpace most of the interceptor fighters sent up to destroy it, and could thus carry out unescorted raids with comparative impunity. (The belief that it could continue to do so against Britain in 1939–40 was very quickly dispelled, and the He 111 was soon given an increased defensive armament and a fighter escort.)

To conserve supplies of the DB 600 engine for the Bf 109 fighter programme, the He 111E was produced next, with a powerplant of two 1,050 hp Junkers Jumo 211A engines. Meanwhile a further civil version, the He 111G, had been developed by Heinkel. Instead of the semi-elliptical wings used on earlier versions, the He 111G introduced, new, straight-tapered wings which were easier to manufacture. No customers appeared for this model, but the new-style wings were introduced on the He 111F bomber variant which was the next to enter production. Both the E and F versions saw service in the Spanish Civil War, bringing to seventy-five the total number of He 111-type aircraft to take part in this conflict. Just before the outbreak of World War 2, the new He 111P had begun to enter service. This had a completely redesigned nose section, of continuous-curve contours (i.e. with no 'step' for the cockpit) and mounting a ball-type gun turret in the extreme nose, offset slightly to starboard. By 3 September 1939 total output of the He 111A/B/D/F/P variants had reached almost a thousand aircraft, and production was to mount rapidly during the war years. The major version of that period was the He 111H, which is described together with other wartime models in the *Bombers 1939–45* volume in this series.

49 Bristol Blenheim

Origins of the Blenheim can be traced back to the Bristol 135 twin-engined monoplane designed by F. S. Barnwell of the Bristol Aeroplane Co in the summer of 1933. This aircraft was not actually built as such, but an example of the basically similar Bristol 142, with 650 hp Mercury VIS.2 instead of 500 hp Aquila engines, was sold to Lord Rothermere, proprietor of the *Daily Mail* newspaper, who named it *Britain First* and later presented it to the nation. It flew for the first time on 12 April 1935 and exhibited a top speed of 307 mph (494 km/hr). Under Air Ministry ownership it received the serial number K7557, and discussions began almost immediately on the question of adapting the design as a high-speed medium bomber. Specification

28/35 was issued to cover this development, and one hundred and fifty aircraft were ordered 'off the drawing board' without a separate bomber prototype. The first production aircraft was K7033, which flew for the first time on 25 June 1936, by which time the bomber had been named Blenheim Mk I with the Bristol Type number 142M. The first squadron deliveries of the new type were made in March 1937, to No 114 Squadron at Wyton, Huntingdonshire. Soon after the first Blenheim had flown, additional contracts began to be placed, both by the RAF and by foreign customers, and by 1939 (when production switched to the long-nosed Blenheim IV – see *Bombers 1939–45*) a total of one thousand two hundred and eighty Mk I's had been completed. Production was shared by Avro and Rootes factories, which built two hundred and fifty and three hundred and thirty-six respectively. The Mk I Blenheim reached its peak of service about the autumn of 1938, when it equipped sixteen U.K.-based RAF bomber squadrons – Nos 21, 34, 44, 57, 61, 62, 82, 90, 101, 104, 107, 108, 110, 114, 139 and 144. It also began to equip overseas stations from early 1938, but had been almost completely replaced in home squadrons by the Blenheim IV by the outbreak of World War 2. At this time the RAF had on charge one thousand and seven Blenheim I's, most of them abroad in Aden, Egypt, India, Iraq and Singapore. The total also included, however, one hundred and forty-seven examples of the Blenheim IF, a stop-gap day fighter version converted from the standard bomber by installing a pack with four 0·303 in Browning machine-guns underneath the forward fuselage. As a day fighter, the Blenheim IF was not an outstanding success, but with the addition of airborne interception radar in 1940 it became a useful night fighter in the early years of the war. Foreign sales and manufacture of the Blenheim I included exports to Finland (eighteen), Greece (six, ex-RAF), Rumania (thirteen), Turkey (thirty) and Yugoslavia (two, plus a further twenty ex-RAF aircraft). In addition, fifty-five Blenheim I's were built under licence in Finland, and the Ikarus factory in Yugoslavia had completed sixteen (of a total of forty laid down) before its production was interrupted by the German invasion and the remaining airframes destroyed to prevent them from falling into enemy hands.

50 Tupolev SB-2

Bomber design made comparatively little advance during the first dozen or so years after the end of World War 1. Then, in quick succession, there appeared independently in several countries a handful of designs for sleek, twin-engined monoplane bombers with retractable undercarriages offering performances well in excess of most fighters then in service. They included the Blenheim, the Martin 139 and the Heinkel He 111, and a close contemporary of this trio was the SB-2 or ANT-40, designed by A. A. Arkhangelski of the Tupolev design bureau. It was evolved from his earlier ANT-21 and ANT-29 twin-engined fighters to meet a 1933 specification, and had a smooth-skinned semi-monocoque airframe of extremely clean lines. Two prototypes were built, which were powered respectively with 700 hp M-25 radial and 750 hp M-100 Vee-type engines for comparative purposes. The first flight was made on 7 October 1934 by the former of these two machines, the M-100 prototype following it into the air on 30 December 1934. Both met all the requirements of the official specification, but the M-100 version exceeded them by such a generous margin that this model was selected to become the SB-2 for series production. This began very quickly after the completion of state acceptance trials in mid-1935, and early in the following year the first SB-2's began to enter squadron service with the Soviet Air Force. In 1936 the 860 hp M-100A engine became the standard powerplant, but two years later the replacement of this unit by the 960 hp M-103, in a much-improved cowling, brought the new designation SB-2 *bis* to describe the aircraft in its latest form. The SB-2 series was built in substantial numbers, and in addition to those equipping medium bomber units in the U.S.S.R. over two hundred saw operational service in support of the Spanish Republican forces during 1936–39 and with the Chinese Air Force when that country was invaded by Japan. Unarmed civil transport versions were used on regular services by Aeroflot, the Soviet state airline, from 1938 onward. These were designated PS-40 and PS-41, corresponding respectively to the SB-2 and SB-2 *bis*. Although obsolescent by the outbreak of World War 2, the Tupolev bombers continued to perform useful service, latterly as night bombers, until after the German invasion of the U.S.S.R. in December 1941. They were particularly prominent in the campaigns in Finland, where they fought both for and against the Finnish Air Force. Thirty Soviet-built SB-2s, with Avia-built HS 12 Ydrs engines, were supplied to Czechoslovakia in 1937, where one hundred and eleven similar aircraft were subsequently built under licence by the Aero and Avia factories. Over forty of these aircraft were later transferred to the Bulgarian Air Force during World War 2, and most of the remainder were acquired by the *Luftwaffe*. Overall Soviet production of SB-2 variants, which included two hundred SB-RK (or Ar-2) dive-bombers with reduced-area wings, has been quoted as reaching a total of six thousand six hundred and sixty-six, with a peak output in 1937 of thirteen aircraft per day.

51 **Douglas B-18**

As the contours of its wing and tail surfaces so plainly indicate, the Douglas B-18 medium bomber was a military derivative of the DC-2 commercial airliner. These features, together with the twin-Cyclone powerplant, were combined with a new-design fuselage accommodating a 6-man crew and a substantial internal bomb load, in a private-venture prototype given the manufacturer's designation DB-1 (Douglas Bomber 1). The DB-1 was one of three designs (another being the four-engined Boeing 299, forerunner of the B-17) submitted in response to a 1934 USAAC requirement for a successor to the Martin B-10. Army trials began in August 1935, resulting in the adoption of both the Boeing and the Douglas designs, the latter receiving a contract for one hundred and thirty-three B-18 bombers in January 1936. The DB-1 prototype was accepted as the first aircraft of this batch, the subsequent machines being essentially similar except for an increased gross weight resulting from the installation of military equipment. The final aircraft on this first contract, completed late in 1937, differed in having a power-operated nose turret installed experimentally, and was designated DB-2. In June 1937 the U.S. Army Air Corps placed a further contract for one hundred and seventy-seven Douglas bombers. These aircraft, and forty of an additional seventy-eight on option, were completed as B-18A's, having uprated Cyclone engines of 1,000 hp (compared with 930 hp in the original B-18), a modified dorsal turret and a redesigned nose section. The former snub-nosed contours of the B-18 were replaced by a longer and extensively-glazed section, of which the upper portion, housing the bomb-aimer, protruded well forward of the lower. Production continued through 1937–38, and the Douglas type was well established as a standard U.S. Army bomber well before America's entry into World War 2, serving *inter alia* with the 5th and 11th Bombing Groups. Early in 1940 a further twenty B-18A bombers were built for the Royal Canadian Air Force. Given the manufacturer's designation DB-280, they were named Digby I by the RCAF, which employed them as convoy escorts or anti-submarine patrol aircraft. A similar maritime role was allotted to those in U.S. service in 1942, when one hundred and twenty-two conversions were made to B-18B standard. Modifications included removing most or all of the nose glazing, in some cases installing a radome in the extreme nose and in others adding an extended tail-cone containing submarine detection gear. Two aircraft of this type were supplied to the Brazilian Air Force for duties over South American waters. The B-18 (sometimes referred to, unofficially, as the Bolo) ended its days as a paratroop training aircraft.

52 Dornier Do 23

Despite its later numerical designation, the Dornier Do 23 actually preceded its more illustrious stablemate, the Do 17, into production and service with the *Luftwaffe*. In fact its origins go back to 1931, to an aircraft then known as the Do F which flew for the first time on 7 May 1932. This was powered by two 550 hp Siemens-built Bristol Jupiter radial engines, and featured a retractable main landing gear. A less obvious feature, at least prior to the official disclosure of the *Luftwaffe*'s existence in 1935, was that the gun emplacements, bomb racks and other military items were delivered separately and secretly, while the Do 11C (as the production version was known) was itself delivered as an 'innocent' civil aeroplane ostensibly intended for freight transport duties with the German railways. The Do 11C was contemporary with the Ju 52/3m in forming the initial equipment of *Luftwaffe* bomber squadrons, but was a much less satisfactory aeroplane. Attempts to eliminate some of its worst characteristics led to the Do 11D, with modified, shorter-span wings, and the Do 11C's in service were also converted to this standard. The Do 13, whose prototype flew on 13 February 1933, was a simplified version with 750 hp BMW VI engines which went into production as the Do 13C; but this continued to suffer from deficiencies in the wing structure and was in turn replaced by the Do 23. The Do 23 offered a strengthened airframe, a further reduction in wing span, and small auxiliary fins mounted below the tailplane. Production began in 1934 with the Do 23F, and was quickly followed by the Do 23G, which became the principal service version built. However, the Do 23 was not destined for a long service life as a bomber, being replaced by the Do 17, Ju 86 and He 111 from 1937, after which it was relegated to second-line duties, including training. On these it remained in use during the early years of World War 2, when one of its tasks was the 'degaussing' of Allied sea mine-fields. Wartime use was also made of some of the earlier Do 11D's, transferred by Germany to the Bulgarian Air Force.

53 Caproni Ca 309/310 series

Two prototype aircraft were designed in 1936 by Ing Cesare Pallavicino of the former Cantieri Aeronautici Bergamaschi, which had become the Compania Aeronautica Bergamasca, a part of the Caproni group, in 1931. These aircraft were the Ca 309 Ghibli (Desert Wind) and the Ca 310 Libeccio (South-west Wind), both designed as 'colonial' aircraft for policing and general-purpose duties in Italy's territories overseas. The Ca 309 was the simpler design of the two, having a non-retractable undercarriage and being powered by two 185 hp Alfa Romeo 115 inverted-Vee engines which gave it a maximum speed of 155 mph (250 km/hr) for a gross weight of 6,067 lb (2,752 kg). It was built in several modest series, which were employed chiefly in North Africa in the roles of light reconnaissance-bomber or 6-seat passenger transport. One version, the Ca 309 Serie VI, was equipped with a 20 mm cannon mounted in the nose and could be employed as a close-support aircraft. The Ca 310 employed the same basic wing as the Ca 309, but was powered by 450 hp Piaggio P.VIIC.16 radial engines whose nacelles also housed the retractable main landing gear.

Although a cleaner aircraft aerodynamically than the Ca 309, and possessed of a much superior performance, the Ca 310 was not adopted for service by the *Regia Aeronautica*, but served extensively with the air forces of other nations. These included the Spanish Nationalist air arm, and those of Croatia, Hungary, Norway and Yugoslavia. A twin-float version, the Ca 310 *Idro*, was produced in prototype form, and another experimental development, known originally as the Ca 310 *bis*, later became the prototype for the Ca 311 production version. This featured an enlarged and extensively glazed nose section and was powered by 500 hp P.VIIC.35 engines. Small batches were built as light bombers for the *Regia Aeronautica*. A further powerplant change, to 700 hp P.XVI RC 35 engines, resulted in the Ca 312. This, like the Ca 311, was produced with both 'stepped' and 'unstepped' windscreens, the former variants being designated Ca 311M and Ca 312M. The Ca 312 was employed primarily for communications or training duties in Italian service, and a few were exported to the Royal Norwegian Air Force. The series ended with two wartime variants, the Ca 313 and Ca 314, combined production of which totalled about one thousand aircraft. These both deviated from the previously standard-span wings, those of the Ca 313 being slightly shorter and those of the Ca 314 slightly longer. Both were powered by Isotta-Fraschini Delta RC 35 engines and had a heavier armament and bomb load than earlier types in the series. Production of the Ca 313 included eighty-four for Sweden; the Ca 314 was employed chiefly as a close-support aircraft or on naval patrol, escort or torpedo-carrying missions during World War 2.

54 Handley Page Harrow

Handley Page, like Bristol, produced a prototype to the C.26/31 Specification for a new RAF bomber-transport. Both went into production, the Bristol 130 as the Bombay (see next entry) and the H.P.51 in modified form as the H.P.54 Harrow. Configuration of the two designs was very similar, the H.P. 51 being immediately more noticeable by its more pronounced wing taper and roughly triangular twin fins and rudders. The H.P. 51 prototype (J9833) was powered by two 700 hp Armstrong Siddeley Tiger radial engines, and utilised the fuselage from an earlier (1932) design, the H.P. 43; it flew for the first time on 8 May 1935. Although it underwent a degree of subsequent modification, the H.P. 51 itself never entered production, but its design formed the basis of the H.P. 54, which was essentially a refined version of the design with all-metal wings and two 830 hp Bristol Pegasus X engines. Its capacity was 20 troops – four less than the Bombay – but in the bomber role it could carry a 3,000 lb (1,361 kg) internal bomb load, half as much again as the Bristol type. No separate prototype of the H.P. 54 was built, and the design was actually evolved originally to meet the night bomber Specification B.3/34. However, its first production contract was to meet the bomber-transport requirement, and the first aircraft to fly was a production Harrow I, K6933. Thirty-eight of the first hundred Harrows ordered were to Mk I standard, with Pegasus X engines, and delivery of these began in April 1937 to No 214 Squadron at Feltwell. Other bomber squadrons to receive Harrows included Nos 37, 75, 115 and 215. Production continued with the Mk II, of which sixty-two were completed. This model of the Harrow was powered by 925 hp Pegasus XX engines and had power-operated gun turrets in the nose and tail; deliveries were completed by the end of 1937.

In 1939 all Harrow squadrons converted to Wellingtons, and most of the Handley Pages were subsequently transferred to transport duties with No 1680 flight, from which was formed No 271 Squadron in March 1940. In the transport role the Harrow continued to serve until late in 1944. At least twelve aircraft had their nose and tail gun positions replaced by smooth fairings; these were known by the name Sparrow and were still in service as ambulance aircraft at the end of World War 2. A number of Harrows were operated on night defence early in the war with No 93 Squadron, using the 'Pandora' system of aerial mine-laying to intercept German night bombers. The original Harrow I and two late-production Mk II's were assigned to Flight Refuelling Ltd in

1939, by whom they were used (bearing civil registrations G-AFRG, 'RH and 'RL) as tanker aircraft in the flight refuelling experiments with the Imperial Airways C class flying boats *Cabot* and *Caribou* which made the first transatlantic air mail flights in August and September 1939. The Harrow I from this trio was subsequently acquired by the Royal Canadian Air Force.

55   Bristol Bombay

The Bristol Type 130, later to become the Bombay, was produced to meet the requirements of Air Ministry Specification C.26/31, which called for a bomber-transport aircraft to replace the ageing Vickers Valentia troop transports then in service at RAF stations in the Middle East and India. The primary requirement was for a transport to carry 24 fully-armed troops, which could also serve as a 4-seat bomber with a 2,000 lb (907 kg) internal bomb load. In March 1933 Bristol received a contract for a single prototype of the Type 130 design, and this aircraft (K3583) flew for the first time on 23 June 1935. Powered by two 750 hp Pegasus IIM.3 radial engines, it was the largest aircraft then built at Bristol's Filton factory, and its broad, large-span wings were of unusually robust construction. Flight development was somewhat protracted, but a contract was eventually placed in 1937 for eighty production aircraft known as Bombay Mk I. By this time a number of improvements had been introduced on the prototype,

including 890 hp Pegasus XXII engines and hydraulically-operated nose and tail turrets of Bristol design. The Bristol factory being fully occupied with production of the Blenheim bomber, production of the Bombay (to Specification 47/36) was delegated to Short Bros and Harland Ltd in Belfast. Later, the number required was reduced to fifty. The first production Bombay flew in March 1939, and the first squadron deliveries (to No 216 Squadron in Egypt) were made six months later. They also equipped Nos 117, 267 and 271 Squadrons of the RAF. The majority of Bombays served operationally in the North African and Sicily/Italy theatres, where their duties included night bombing on the 'Benghazi Milk Run', supply transport and casualty evacuation; one Bombay crew alone carried six thousand casualty cases. They were finally withdrawn from service in August 1944 and officially declared redundant three months later.

56   Mitsubishi Ki-2

In September 1932 the Japanese Army Air Force issued a specification for a 3-seat bomber, capable of carrying a maximum bomb load of 1,102 lb (500 kg) and powered by two 450 hp Nakajima radial engines. This specification was based upon the results of evaluating the German Junkers K-37, an example of which had been donated to the JAAF at the beginning of the year and had later served operationally, with the name *Aikoku* (Patriot) No 1, in

Manchuria. Mitsubishi, having had experience already of building large bomber aircraft – notably the Ki-20, based on the Junkers G-38, and its own Ki-1 design, of which it built one hundred and eighteen – was selected to construct a prototype to meet the new requirement. Proposals by Mitsubishi to utilise its own M-4 engines in the prototype, and to incorporate such features as an oleo-strut landing gear and a barbette-type installation for the nose gun, were rejected by the JAAF, and the first prototype was thus built strictly to the specification. It was completed in May 1933, and during its flight test programme at Kagamigahara airfield proved to have excellent handling characteristics. An extremely slender rear fuselage had been designed for the first prototype, in order to give the dorsal gunner the maximum field of fire; but after this machine was damaged when landing after an engine failure it was decided that the rear fuselage of the second prototype should follow the rather more substantial pattern of the Junkers K-37. In this form, the Mitsubishi bomber was accepted late in 1933 for Army service as the Type 93 light bomber, or Ki-2. The initial version was known as the Ki-2-1, and remained in production until 1936, by which time one hundred and thirteen had been built. It was then superseded on the assembly lines by the Ki-2-2, a developed version powered by two 550 hp Type 95 radial engines. In this model, Mitsubishi did introduce the features rejected four years previously by the JAAF, for the Ki-2-2 had a retractable main landing gear, an oval-shaped nose turret, enclosed accommodation for the pilot and front gunner, and an internal bomb bay capable of holding twenty 33 lb (15 kg) bombs. With these and other detail refinements the Ki-2-2 was some 19 mph (30 km/hr) faster than the previous model; during 1937–38, sixty-one of this version were built. The Ki-2 was used operationally in the early stages of the war with China, notably in the Manchurian and North China theatres. After withdrawal from first-line service they continued to serve as bombing crew trainers, in which capacity a few were still in existence when Japan entered World War 2.

57 Mitsubishi G3M

The Japanese Naval Air Force competitions of 1934 were the first to produce new equipment of a significantly modern standard, capable of favourable comparison with the best contemporary western designs. In particular, they gave rise to the Mitsubishi A5M carrier-based monoplane fighter and a land-based twin-engined medium bomber from the same manufacturer, the G3M. Mitsubishi's association with the design and construction of Junkers-type aircraft in the early 1930s was reflected in the new bomber, which externally at least bore more than a superficial resemblance to the Ju 86. The temporary designation Ka-15 was originally given to the Mitsubishi project, which was based on an earlier project, the Ka-9, and designed by Professor Kiro Honjo as a cantilever mid-wing monoplane with a circular-section fuselage, flush-riveted skin and retractable main landing gear. The first Ka-15 prototype, powered by two 750 hp Hiro Type 91 Vee-type engines, was completed in July 1935 and made its first flight shortly afterwards. A further twenty prototype/pre-production Ka-15's were built, three of them with Hiro engines and the remainder with Mitsubishi Kinsei 2 or 3 radials of 680 or 790 hp, which offered an improved performance. They were given the JNAF designation G3M1, subdivided unofficially into G3M1a (Hiro engines), G3M1b (Kinsei engines) and G3M1c (those with glazed nose areas). Twelve G3M1's were used for service trials, and while these were still in progress the construction of an initial production batch of G3M1's with Kinsei 3 engines was authorised. Thirty-four of these were built, this model then being supplanted by the G3M2, which was destined to become the principal version. Mitsubishi built two basic variants of the G3M2. These were the Model 21, with higher-powered Kinsei engines, increased fuel tankage and modified dorsal turrets; and the Model 22, with a revised armament installation which included the elimination of the retractable ventral turret. Three hundred and forty-three Model 21's were manufactured by Mitsubishi from 1937–39, followed by two hundred and thirty-eight examples of the Model 22 from 1939–41. Building of the G3M2 was also undertaken by Nakajima, whose Koizumi factory continued to build the bomber after the parent company had ceased production in favour of the later G4M design. Altogether, Nakajima built a total of four hundred and twelve G3M's, a proportion of which were G3M3's with 1,300 hp Kinsei 53 engines and a further increase in fuel capacity. The G3M entered JNAF service early in 1937, and two squadrons were equipped with these bombers when the Sino-Japanese conflict began in July of that year. They soon made world-wide news with their transoceanic raids from Omura (Japan) and Taipei (Formosa) on the Chinese cities of Hangkow and Nanking; but the Japanese were misled by the poor fighter opposition (like their later allies, the Germans, in Spain) into thinking that the bombers could operate safely without a fighter escort. Additional fighters were summoned urgently from Japan – but in 1940 the G3M bombers found themselves acting as escort to China of the first two squadrons of A6M2 Zero fighters! Upon the outbreak of the Pacific War in December 1941 the JNAF had a first- and second-line strength of approximately two hundred and fifty G3M2 bombers; the type took part in the initial attacks on the Philippine Islands, and in the sinking of the British warships *Prince of Wales* and *Repulse*. Prior to the war some two dozen G3M2's were converted for use as civil transport aircraft, a role repeated during wartime by converting a number of G3M1 and G3M2 aircraft into L3Y1 and L3Y2 military transports.

58 **Dornier Do 17**

Three prototypes of the Do 17, all with single fins and rudders, were built to meet a requirement by the German airline, Deutsche Lufthansa, for a high-speed mailplane also capable of carrying six passengers. The first of these prototypes made its maiden flight in the autumn of 1934. The extreme slimness of the Do 17's fuselage, which later earned it such nicknames as 'Eversharp' and 'Flying Pencil', proved its undoing as a commercial transport, for passengers could reach their seats in the narrow fuselage only with extreme difficulty. Some time after its rejection by DLH, however, the *Reichsluftfahrtministerium* decided to evaluate the Dornier design as a possible contender in its quest for a new medium bomber for the *Luftwaffe*. Additional prototypes were ordered by the RLM, the first of which (the Do 17V4) appeared with the twin-fin assembly that was to become standard on the subsequent production aircraft. The fuselage, somewhat shorter than those of the original trio, was of metal construction, as were the metal-and-fabric-covered wings. The Do 17V4, V6 and V7 were powered, like the first three aircraft, with 660 hp BMW VI Vee-type engines, and the V7 was also the first to have armament installed. Powerplant of the V5 was a pair of 770 hp Hispano-Suiza 12Y engines. Production was initiated late in 1936, the first series-built

models being the Do 17E-1 bomber (750 hp BMW VI engines) and the Do 17F-1 long-range reconnaissance bomber; both were in *Luftwaffe* squadron service by mid-1937, the first recipients being units of KG 153 and KG 155. In July 1937 the Do 17 made a spectacular public debut at the International Military Aircraft Competition at Zurich, when it completely overshadowed in performance the French Dewoitine D 510, then regarded widely as the best single-seat fighter being built in Europe – although by this time Germany's own Messerschmitt Bf 109 fighter was of course also entering production. But neither this nor the fact that the Zurich demonstrator was a specially-stripped prototype (the Do 17V8) with boosted engines could deny the fact the *Luftwaffe* now possessed a highly impressive new medium bomber, and in 1938 Dornier 17's were among the new types of German warplane sent to try out their strength with the *Luftwaffe*'s Condor Legion fighting in the Spanish Civil War. The next series versions were the Do 17M bomber (900 hp Bramo Fafnir 323A engines) and the reconnaissance-bomber Do 17P, which had 865 hp BMW 132N radial engines; these entered production late in 1937, replacing respectively the E and F models. Meanwhile, foreign interest, aroused by the Do 17's display at Zurich, resulted in the development of the Do 17K export version, ordered by the Yugoslav Air Force and fitted at their request with 986 hp Gnome-Rhône 14N radial engines. With this powerplant the speed and range were improved, and maximum internal bomb load was increased to 2,205 lb (1,000 kg) compared with the 1,764 lb (800 kg) of the Do 17E-1. Twenty German-built Do 17K's were sold to Yugoslavia, and others were built by the State Aircraft Factory near Belgrade. When the country was invaded by Germany in April 1941, about seventy Do 17K's were in Yugoslav Air Force service. A total of five hundred and eighty Do 17E/F/M/P production aircraft had been delivered by mid-September 1938. Early in 1938 development began of the experimental Do 17R and Do 17S series; these in turn led to the Do 17Z, which entered production in the autumn of that year. About five hundred and twenty-five of this model, in various sub-series, were built before Do 17 production finally ended in 1940.

59   Junkers Ju 86

The Ju 86 was a contemporary of the Heinkel He 111, both aircraft being designed in 1934 to a joint military and civil requirement for a multi-engined aircraft capable of serving both as a bomber and as a commercial transport. Five prototypes were ordered initially, of which the first made its maiden flight on 4 November 1934, powered by two Siemens radial engines pending the availability of the Junkers Jumo 205 engines for which it had been designed. These were installed in the Ju 86V2 (D-ABUK), which flew for the first time in April 1935. A pre-series batch of thirteen

Ju 86-A-o's, for service trials, was followed by the first deliveries of the Ju 86A-1 model to KG 152 in May/June 1936. These aircraft (about twenty of which were built) had 600 hp Jumo 205C-4 engines and an internal bomb load of 1,764 lb (800 kg). From the A model was developed the Ju 86D-1 (the B and C series having been commercial transports), with increased fuel capacity and an extended fuselage tail-cone to improve stability; but the Jumo engine proved to be unsuitable for the type of operations the bomber was to perform. Installation of the Pratt & Whitney Hornet radial engine or its German licence-built counterpart, the 810 hp BMW 132F, in two Ju 86D's led to the adoption of a version with the latter engines (the Ju 86E) to supersede the D model in production. The Ju 86E began to enter service in the late summer of 1937; about fifty were built, some of them with 865 hp BMW 132N engines. A further forty aircraft, begun as Ju 86E's, were completed as Ju 86G's, having redesigned front fuselages with the cockpit further forward to improve the pilot's view for take-off or landing. From the autumn of 1938 (when there were two hundred and thirty-five Ju 86A/D/E/G bombers in service) the type began to be withdrawn from first-line *Luftwaffe* units in favour of the He 111 and Do 17. However, before this, the aircraft had also been the subject of foreign military orders. Three Hornet-engined bombers (designated Ju 86K-1) were evaluated by Sweden in the winter of 1936–37, these trials being followed by the delivery of twenty (designated B 3A) with Swedish-built Bristol Pegasus III engines and a further seventeen (B 3B) with Pegasus XII's. The German designations for these were Ju 86K-4 and K-5 respectively. The Swedish Saab company then built under licence sixteen Ju 86K-13's, these being either B 3C's (with Pegasus XXIV engines) or B 3D's (Pegasus XIX). Small batches of Hornet-engined Ju 86K's were also supplied to Chile and Portugal, and twenty-four with 870 hp Gnome-Rhône 14K-series engines were built under licence in Hungary; in addition, eighteen Ju 86 airliners of the South African Airways fleet were taken over by the SAAF in 1939 and re-equipped as bombers. After the outbreak of World War 2 Junkers evolved the Ju 86P, a high-altitude bomber and photographic reconnaissance version with redesigned nose, extended-span wings and Jumo 207A engines; and the Ju 86R, which had a further-increased wing span and 1,000 hp Jumo 207B engines. Most P and R series aircraft were produced by converting existing airframes of earlier models.

60 Breguet 690 series

Although in its three basic production versions the Breguet 690 was built for service chiefly in the light assault-bomber role, it was in fact designed as a contender for a 3-seat fighter competition, although it did not after all take part in the contest. The prototype Bre 690 was completed in May 1937, after some two years in the design and construction stages; but since Breguet had opted out of the 1936 nationalisation of the French aviation industry, and the Potez 63 fighter production programme (see *Fighters 1939–45*) by then had first claim on the supply of Hispano-Suiza 14AB radial engines, it was not until 23 March 1938 that Georges Ricard's design was able to make its first flight. The Bre 690 was a handsome aircraft, whose extremely clean lines marked a complete departure from the ugly angularity of earlier Breguet products, and its performance during flight trials proved it too good an aeroplane to be overlooked. In June 1938 Breguet received an initial contract for one hundred examples of a production version, designated Bre 691AB.2 and intended for the 2-seat attack-bomber role. These were powered by 750 hp HS 14AB engines, and the first squadron deliveries were made in October 1939 to GBA I/54 at Orléans-Bricy. In the event, only seventy-eight Bre 691's were completed. One of these became the prototype for the next production model, the Bre 693, flying for the first time on 25 October 1939 after being fitted with a pair of 700 hp Gnome-Rhône 14M radial engines. One hundred and twenty-six Bre 693's were built in France. Plans were laid for nine of these aircraft, and thirty-two Bre 694's (a 3-seat reconnaissance variant with 710 hp GR 14M engines) to be built under licence by SABCA in Belgium, but these were negated by the German invasion in 1940. Sweden also ordered twelve Bre 694's, but later cancelled the contract. The final French production model was the Bre 695, which followed the refitting of the original Bre 690-01 prototype with 825 hp American Twin Wasp Junior engines. Fifty of this version were ordered from July 1939, but the first production example did not fly until late in April 1940 and it is not certain that all were completed. The Breguet 692, which remained a project only, was to have had more powerful Gnome-Rhône engines. Single prototypes were completed of the Bre 694 (see above), which was later delivered to the *Aéronavale*, the Bre 696 (2-seat bomber) and Bre 697 ('heavy' fighter), all with variously-powered Gnome-Rhône engines. The Bre 698 dive-bomber, Bre 699 bomber and Bre 700 'heavy' fighter were other projected variants which, as events turned out, were never built.

61 Caproni Ca 101 series

The Ca 101, itself a derivative of Caproni's earlier Ca 97, became the design basis for several subsequent trimotor designs, chief among which were the Ca 111 and the Ca 133. Like the somewhat later Ca 309, it also was employed primarily as a general-purpose 'colonial' aircraft for service in Italian overseas territories. It first entered service with the *Regia Aeronautica* shortly before the Italian invasion of Ethiopia, when it was allocated a more belligerent role with the *Stormi da Bombardamento* as an attack aircraft, in addition to performing as a supply transporter ambulance. The Ca 101 was produced for civilian as well as military use, and in the former capacity was fitted with a wide variety of alternative powerplants during its career. Most of the military examples, however, were powered by the Alfa Romeo D2 engine, usually uncowled. The Ca 101 was a sturdily-built aeroplane, and its thick, broad wings in particular combined great strength and lifting ability. It had largely disappeared from *Regia Aeronautica* service by the end of the Ethiopian campaign, in favour of later developments of the design. Small numbers were built of the Ca 102, which was essentially a twin-engined counterpart of the Ca 101. One Ca 102 was completed with four engines mounted in tandem pairs, and was flown by the 62° *Sperimentale Bombardieri Pesanti* (Experimental Heavy Bomber Squadron). The Ca 111 retained the essentials of the Ca 101 airframe, but despite its great size and weight was powered by a single engine only – the 950 hp Isotta-Fraschini Asso 750 RC radial. It appeared both in landplane form and as the Ca 111 *bis Idro* twin-float seaplane, the former serving alongside the Ca 101 in the Ethiopian campaign. It remained in service during World War 2, one example still surviving at the time of the Italian surrender in 1943. Ethiopia also saw the debut of the Ca 133, a slightly-enlarged development powered by three 450 hp Piaggio P.VIIC.14 radial engines in NACA-type cowlings. When Italy entered World War 2, fourteen

Squadriglie da Bombardamento Terrestre in East Africa were flying Capronis of this type, and others were used in the Italian invasion of Albania or as transports or ambulances in North Africa.

62 Junkers Ju 52/3m

Probably the most famous trimotor aeroplanes ever built were the Fokker airliners of the later 1920s, and the Junkers Ju 52/3m. Both originated as commercial transport designs, and both had their military counterparts, but the military service of the German aircraft was by far the greater. It originated in 1928 with the Ju 52, which was powered by a single 800 hp Junkers L-88 Vee-type engine and flew for the first time on 13 October 1930. Some eighteen months later Junkers flew the first example of a three-engined development of this design, powered by a trio of 575 hp BMW-built Pratt & Whitney Hornet radial engines; this version was given the designation Ju 52/3m, and the single-engined version was retrospectively distinguished as the Ju 52/1m. The trimotor entered production in 1934, and quickly became popular as a commercial transport with Deutsche Lufthansa and a number of foreign operators, notably in Europe and South America. Some, fitted with a twin-float landing gear, were designated Ju 52/3mW (for *Wasser=water*). With the creation of the *Luftwaffe*, the aircraft was adopted for military service as interim equipment for the first bomber squadrons, and four hundred and fifty were built as 4-seat bombers. These were known as Ju 52/3mg3e's, and saw their first operational service in the late summer of 1936 when twenty of them were among the first German aircraft sent to Spain after the outbreak of the Civil War. By the end of the following year, however, the Junkers type had been superseded as a *Luftwaffe* bomber by such later types as the He 111 and Do 17, and was largely transferred to troop transport duties, which were more appropriate to its capabilities. In this latter role the aircraft customarily retained its dorsal-mounted 7·9 mm MG 15 machine-gun, but more often than not the second gun and its retractable ventral 'dustbin' mounting were omitted. Manufacture of the Ju 52/3m in Germany was to continue until mid-1944, and the overall production total (including civil aircraft and quantities built by Amiot in France and CASA in Spain) reached four thousand eight hundred and forty-five. German production totalled five hundred and seventy-five up to the end of 1939 and a further two thousand six hundred and fifty-nine thereafter. Successive military variants were distinguished by suffixes from g3e to g14e, signifying either the specific role of a particular model (e.g. transport, ambulance, mine clearance), the installation of later variants of the BMW 132 engine (licence version of the American Hornet) or miscellaneous structural alterations. The wartime career of the Ju 52/3m is described in the *Bombers 1939–45* volume in this series.

63 Savoia-Marchetti S.M.81 Pipistrello (Bat)

In 1934 the SIAI Savoia-Marchetti produced an 18-passenger commercial transport aircraft, the S.M.73, powered by three 700 hp Piaggio Stella IX RC radial engines, which was built for Italian and foreign airline service. Later in the same year a military bomber-transport version, the S.M.81, also made its first appearance. After extensive evaluation of the prototype and a small batch of pre-production machines by the *Regia Aeronautica*, it was ordered into large-scale production; in addition to the parent company, the CMASA and Piaggio factories also built the S.M.81 and component manufacture was undertaken by a very large number of other companies within the Italian aircraft industry. Because of the widespread nature of the production programme, it was found expedient to adopt a number of alternative powerplants; chief among these were the 650 or 680 hp Alfa Romeo 125 RC 35 or 126 RC 34, the 650 hp Gnome-Rhône 14K, and the 670 hp Piaggio P.X RC 35, all being radial engines. An experimental version, the S.M.81 *bis*, was also built, with two 840 hp Isotta-Fraschini Asso XI RC Vee-type engines and a glazed bombing station in place of a third engine in the nose. This, however, did not progress beyond the prototype stage. The S.M.81 began to enter service with Italian *Stormi da Bombardamento Terrestre* (Land-based Bomber Squadrons) early in 1935, and twelve *Stormi* were still equipped with these aircraft at the outbreak of World War 2. At least one *Stormo da Bombardamento Marittimo* was also equipped with the S.M.81. First deliveries were made to units based in Italy, but a considerable part of the S.M.81's pre-war service was carried out in Italian North and East Africa and Ethiopia, beginning with the arrival of the first squadron in Eritrea late in 1935. At the end of July 1936 the S.M.81 became one of the first foreign aircraft types to arrive in Spain in support of General Franco's Nationalist forces, having previously taken an active part in the Italian invasion of Ethiopia. In this it was employed both as a bomber and a transport, and one S.M.81 (named *Tartaruga* = tortoise) was later used as the personal transport of Mussolini. With the entry into service of the S.M.79 *Sparviero* (see *Bombers 1939–45*) the S.M.81 was gradually phased out of service with Italian-based first-line squadrons, but as indicated above it continued to equip several units in Africa until after Italy's entry into World War 2, at which point just over three hundred serviceable Pipistrellos were still on strength.

64 Fokker F.VII/3m

The original Fokker F.VII was a single-engined high-wing transport, designed by Ing W. Rethel, who later became chief designer of the Arado Flugzeugwerke in Germany. From this aircraft Anthony Fokker and his chief designer, Reinhold Platz, evolved in the mid-1920's a trimotor development which was to become one of the most celebrated transport aircraft ever built. Unlike its near-contemporary, the Junkers Ju 52/3m, the Fokker F.VII/3m was not nearly so successful in its selection for a military career. The first military version, identified as the F.VIIa-3m/M, was powered by three 200 hp uncowled Armstrong Siddeley Lynx radial engines, and was evaluated by the Dutch *Luchtvaartafdeling* (Army Air Service) for potential service in a variety of roles. Chief among these were those of bomber (carrying a 2,204 lb = 1,000 kg bomb load), torpedo-bomber (with a single 1,000 kg torpedo carried externally) and ambulance (with accommodation for six stretchers). These trials, however, brought an order for only ten aircraft, some of which were of the F.VIIb-3m/M version with 300 hp Wright Whirlwind radial engines and wings of increased span. Only three of the ten were retained for the LVA's use in Holland, and were employed for night-flying, bombing training or general-purpose transport duty. The other seven were assigned to the Netherlands Indies Army Air Service, by whom they were employed as bomber-transports. A small batch of F.Viib-3m/M's were built under licence in Poland by the Plage and Laskievicz factory, serving initially as bombers and subsequently as transports. These were still in service when Poland was invaded in 1939. Single examples were acquired by the RAF and the USAAC for evaluation, but no production orders from these quarters ensued. Three

were constructed under licence in Spain (probably by CASA) prior to the outbreak of the Civil War in 1936. These followed the acquisition of one Dutch-built aircraft from Fokker in 1934. A few airline Fokker F.VIIb-3m's also served in both Republican and Nationalist air force markings during the Civil War, either as transports or as training aircraft.

65 **Tupolev TB-3**
The tradition of the long-range heavy bomber was established early in Russia, with the huge four-engined Sikorsky *Ilya Mourometz* that served with Tsar Nicholas II's Squadron of Flying Ships for nearly three years before the November 1917 Revolution. Eight years later, a decision made by the Central Aero and Hydrodynamic Institute (TsAGI) and the Special Technical Bureau in the U.S.S.R. was to lead to the appearance of another significant Soviet heavy bomber, the TB-3. This was evolved at the design bureau headed by Andrei N. Tupolev, its bureau designation being ANT-6. It was developed from an earlier type, the smaller twin-engined TB-1 (ANT-4) which flew in prototype form in November 1925 and of which two hundred examples were subsequently built. Both the TB-1 and the TB-3 were cantilever monoplanes, of all-metal construction with a corrugated metal skin. The wings were designed by one of Tupolev's leading protégés, Vladimir Petlyakov, and were of tremendous thickness and strength, having five spars and

being built in three sections. The TB-3 prototype was a considerably larger aircraft than its predecessor, and was powered by four 600 hp Curtiss Conqueror Vee-type engines for its first flight on 22 December 1930 – which nearly ended in disaster when the starboard engine throttle levers failed to stay open shortly after take-off. After some two months of test flying the American engines were replaced by a quartet of 730 hp BMW VI engines, the Soviet-built counterpart of which (the 715 hp M-17F) was adopted as the powerplant for the first production examples of the TB-3. Some indication of the rate of production of these huge aircraft is reflected by the numbers which appeared in successive May Day fly-pasts over Moscow; nine in 1932, fifty in 1933 and over two hundred and fifty in 1934. By this time, however, later models had begun to supplant the original version on the production lines. One of the first major changes was to replace the rather low-powered M-17F engines by 830 hp M-34's. A prototype with the latter power-plant passed its acceptance trials in the autumn of 1933, but performance was not improved until these in turn were replaced by M-34R engines fitted with reduction gear. The M-34R version went into production in 1934, followed not long afterwards by an even further-improved model with 970 hp M-34RN geared and supercharged engines. This version could carry a bomb load of 4,409 lb (2,000 kg) over long ranges or a maximum internal and

external load of 12,787 lb (5,800 kg) for short distances – a greater load, with a better performance, than any other heavy bomber then in quantity production. The final power change came in 1935, with the introduction of M-34FRN engines of 900 hp. Numerous structural refinements and modifications were introduced as the production and service life of the TB-3 unfolded. These included the provision of wheel brakes for the original tandem-bogie main wheels in 1933, and in 1937 the adoption of single-wheel main units with 'trouser' fairings round the shock struts; the introduction of fillet fairings at the wing roots; the use of fabric covering for the tail surfaces; and finally, in 1937, the adoption of a smooth skin surface in place of the corrugated type. Armament underwent drastic reduction, from the ten guns carried by the slow-moving TB-3/M-17 version. First to go were the two pairs of guns in nacelle turrets beneath the wings; these were replaced by a new tail-gun position which involved extending the rear fuselage and redesigning the vertical tail surfaces. More efficient ShKAS machine-guns eventually replaced the DA-2 guns fitted to early TB-3's, and in the final model (now carrying only three defensive guns instead of the original ten) manually-operated nose and dorsal turrets replaced the former open positions. The TB-3 was used for cargo and paratroop transport duties (designated G-2) as well as in the bomber role; aircraft of this type did much useful work with Soviet Arctic expeditions, and others were used in 'parasite fighter' experiments. Some eight hundred TB-3's of all versions were built, serving from 1932 until and throughout World War 2.

66 Farman 221 and 222

The first four-engined bomber to enter service with France's *Armée de l'Air*, the Farman 221 had its origins in a requirement issued in 1929 by the *Service Technique Aéronautique* for a BN5 (*Bombardement de Nuit*, 5-seat) replacement for the obsolescent LeO 20 series of bombers. The prototype was the Farman 220–01, which flew for the first time on 26 May 1932; it was derived from the earlier F210/211/212 series of designs, and was powered by four Hispano-Suiza 12 Lbr Vee-type engines, mounted in tandem pairs with each pair driving one tractor and one pusher propeller. This prototype was later handed over to Air France, with whom, as F-ANLG *Centaure*, it flew for many years on airmail services to South America. Meanwhile a second bomber prototype, the F 221-01, had flown in the summer of 1933, differing from its predecessor in having 800 hp Gnome-Rhône 14K radial engines and a redesigned glazed nose section offering a better view. This aircraft set a world altitude record with an 11,023 lb (5,000 kg) payload on 16 June 1934. Only ten production examples of the Farman 221 were built, the first delivery (of five aircraft) being made to the 15e *Escadre de Bombarde-ment* at Avord in the spring of 1936. Meanwhile the F221-01 had been the subject of further development, from which it emerged with a retractable main landing gear and the new designation F222-01. Eleven production examples followed, these being designated F222/1. They were delivered to GB I/15 in April 1937, except for four aircraft which were assigned to the 4e *Escadre* at Tong, in French Indochina. After this initial production batch came twenty-four Farman 222/2's, which differed in having dihedral on the outer wing panels and a lengthened and redesigned nose section. The final sixteen aircraft of this batch were manufactured by the SNCA du Centre, the new organisation formed in the nationalisation of the French aircraft industry by the amalgamation of the Farman and Hanriot companies. Some two dozen Farman 221 or 222 bombers were in service at the outbreak of World War 2 with the 15e *Escadre*, the only formation in France flying this type of aircraft. They were used during the early months of the war for reconnaissance and leaflet 'raids' over Germany. In June 1940 *Groupement* 15, as it was now known, was transferred to the North African theatre where, four months later, it was reclassified as a transport unit. It continued to utilise its Farmans in this new role until their withdrawal in 1944. A small number of F222's also served on maritime patrol duties around the West African coast with units of the *Aéronavale*.

67 Boeing B-17 Fortress

Later to become one of the most famous (and most prolific) bombers ever built, the Boeing Fortress was the outcome of a 1934 USAAC requirement for an offshore anti-shipping bomber. Boeing had already undertaken preliminary design work for a Model 299 bomber project and a transport counterpart, the Model 300; and in August 1934 it began in earnest to develop the former design to meet the Army requirement. The Boeing 299 prototype (X13372), powered by four 750 hp Pratt & Whitney Hornet radial engines, made its first flight on 28 July 1935. Just over three weeks later it made an impressive 2,100 mile (3,380 km) non-stop flight from Seattle to Wright Field to begin its evaluation trials with the USAAC, but it was destroyed in a take-off accident on 30 October 1935. Already, however, the new aircraft had given sufficient promise of its potential worth, and in the following January Boeing received a contract for thirteen Y1B-17 and one Y1B-17A aircraft for more exhaustive service trials. These differed from the prototype in having 930 hp Wright Cyclone engines, those of the Y1B-17A being fitted with turbo-superchargers. Twelve of the Y1B-17's were placed in service with the Army's 2nd Bombardment Group, with whom they remained (simply as B-17's) after the successful completion of their service trials. Due to a conflict of opinion between Army and Navy staffs over the responsibility for protecting the American coastline, it was not until 1938 that the first Fortress production contract was placed – and this was for the comparatively modest quantity of thirty-nine aircraft. These incorporated a number of improvements, notably a modified nose and a larger rudder, and were designated B-17B. Successive production batches included thirty-eight B-17C's (increased armament and a different mark of Cyclone engine), twenty of which were supplied to the Royal Air Force in 1941 as the Fortress Mk I; and forty-two B-17D's, which had a tenth crew member, self-sealing fuel tanks and no external bomb racks. Most of the USAAF's remaining B-17C's were eventually converted to D standard. The last Fortress variant to appear before America's entry into World War 2 was the B-17E, which first flew in September 1941. This involved a more extensive redesign to bring the bomber into line with current requirements. It was the first model to introduce the huge, sail-like fin and rudder that characterised all subsequent Fortresses, and firepower was considerably increased by the installation of power turrets above and below the fuselage, the provision for the first time of a tail gun position and of a multi-gun nose, bringing total defensive armament to thirteen guns. Five hundred and twelve B-17E's were built by Boeing, including forty-five supplied to the RAF as the Fortress IIA. Other wartime variants are described in the *Bombers 1939–45* volume. The early service life of the

B-17 series was punctuated by a number of impressive long-distance flights. These included the flights of six aircraft from Miami to Buenos Aires (5,260 miles = 8,465 km) in 1938, with only one refuelling stop en route, many non-stop coast-to-coast flights across the U.S.A. and another formation flight to Rio de Janeiro in November 1939. In August 1939 the Y1B-17A, carrying an 11,000 lb (4,990 kg) payload, set an altitude record of 34,000 ft (10,363 m) and a 621 mile (1,000 km) closed-circuit speed record of 259·4 mph (417·5 km/hr).

68 Loening OA and OL series

The Loening Aeronautical Engineering Co of New York was founded by Grover C. Loening, an inventive pioneer who had graduated as an aeronautical engineer in 1911 and had in his early days worked with Orville and Wilbur Wright. In the early 1920s he was responsible for a series of amphibious aircraft for the U.S. Army and Navy, beginning with the COA-1 (Corps Observation Amphibian) in 1924. The main feature of these aircraft was that, instead of having a separate fuselage and central float united by struts, the area between these two structures was completely faired in, enabling the internal space thus provided to accommodate working equipment and, at the same time, providing an aerodynamically better shape. This feature was facilitated by use of the inverted-Vee Liberty engine, whose high thrust line permitted the distance from fuselage to float to be kept to a minimum.

The first of two XCOA-1's was flown in July 1924, after which nine COA-1's were built for service trials, fifteen OA-1A's (with modified fins and rudders), nine basically similar OA-1B's, and ten OA-1C's in which the vertical tail was again redesigned. The main landing wheels retracted into the sides of the central float, at the rear of which was a small tail skid, and small stabilising floats were fitted beneath the outer panels of the lower wings. Final Army version was the OA-2, eight of which were built in 1929 and which had more up-to-date Wright V-1460 Tornado engines of 480 hp in place of the 400 hp Libertys. The Navy amphibians began with the OL-1, a 3-seat version powered by a 440 hp Packard 1A-1500 engine; two of these were built. The OL-2 was the Naval counterpart to the COA-1, and five were completed. One of the OL-1's was used to incorporate a number of design improvements, leading to a contract for four more similar aircraft as OL-3's, and six with Liberty engines as OL-4's. There was no OL-5, but twenty-eight examples were ordered of the OL-6. This introduced the tall, angular vertical tail of the OA-1C and was powered by the Packard engine. The XOL-7, with redesigned wings of thicker section, remained only a prototype, but the XOL-8 led to orders for twenty OL-8's and twenty OL-8A's, which introduced, for the first time, a radial engine to the series – the 450 hp Pratt & Whitney Wasp. The OL-8A's had deck arrester gear fitted, but were otherwise similar to the OL-8. Final version was the OL-9, twenty-six of which were built after the amalgamation of Loening with the Keystone Aircraft Corporation; these were preceded by two other machines, designated XHL-1, which were intended for use as 6-passenger ambulance aircraft.

69 Grumman JF/J2F Duck

Much of the early work conducted by the Grumman Aircraft Engineering Corporation after its formation at the end of 1929 was directed towards the evolution of retractable landing gear for U.S. Naval aircraft. In one direction this took practical form in the little FF-1 fighter (see *Fighters 1919–39*). Another aspect of the same approach led to the evolution of amphibious aircraft, through the development of an aircraft float which incorporated a fully-retractable wheel landing gear. Leroy Grumman had formerly been an associate of Grover Loening, and the OL types produced by the latter's company (see previous description) typified the earlier work in this field which Grumman had carried out. After forming his own company, Grumman began the development of a new observation/ utility amphibian which materialised as the XJF-1 prototype, flown for the first time on 4 May 1933 and powered by a 700 hp Pratt & Whitney Twin Wasp Junior radial engine. Twenty-seven production JF-1's were ordered shortly afterward, these having R-1830-62 Twin Wasp engines and an enclosed cockpit for the 2-man crew.

The first deliveries of JF-1's were made in mid-1934 to U.S. Navy Squadron VS-3 in the aircraft carrier USS *Lexington*. Intended originally for utility and communications duties, the JF-1's eventually found themselves employed on a range of tasks which included photographic reconnaissance, target towing, ambulance work and rescue. Fourteen aircraft, similar to the JF-1 except for their internal equipment and 750 hp Wright Cyclone engines, were built as JF-2's for the U.S. Coast Guard. One of these aircraft, flown by Cmdr E. F. Stone, set up a new world speed record for amphibious aircraft of 191·796 mph (308·665 km/hr) on 21 December 1934. Five Cyclone-engined aircraft were acquired by the U.S. Navy as JF-3's, one JF-2 was supplied to the U.S. Marine Corps, and eight similar aircraft were sold to the Argentine Navy. An improved model of the JF design appeared in 1935. First flown on 25 June of that year, this was known as the J2F-1 and was later given the name Duck officially. Improvements were primarily directed towards specific use of the Duck from aircraft carriers of the U.S. Fleet, and included the provision of catapult points and deck arrester gear. The U.S. Navy purchased twenty J2F-1's, which were powered by Cyclone engines. Successive orders for later models, differing in minor detail only, included twenty-one J2F-2's, twenty J2F-3's and thirty-two J2F-4's. A major external change – the long chord NACA-type cowling for the 850 hp Cyclone engine – was evident in the next model, the J2F-5, of which one hundred and forty-four were ordered early in 1941. Grumman factories were from then onward fully occupied in building the F4F fighter, but a further three hundred and thirty Ducks, with the Grumman-style designation J2F-6, were manufactured during 1939–45 by the Columbia Aircraft Corporation with 900 hp Cyclone engines.

70 Nakajima E8N

The 2-seat Nakajima E8N was designed in 1933, emerging as the successful contender in the 8-*Shi* (1933) requirement for a reconnaissance floatplane operable from coastal bases or from major ships of the Imperial Japanese Navy. It was basically a developed version of Nakajima's earlier E4N1 (Type 90) floatplane, the design of which had itself been influenced by the American Vought Corsair observation aircraft of the U.S. Navy. Seven prototype/pre-production aircraft were built, and after comparative trials with rival designs submitted by Aichi and Kawanishi the Nakajima aircraft was selected in the autumn of 1935 for series production. It had two open cockpits, situated in tandem, was powered by a 580 hp Nakajima Kotobuki 2-Kai-I radial engine, and was allocated the JNAF designation E8N1 or Type 95 reconnaissance floatplane. The E8N1 had one forward-firing and one rearward-firing machine-gun, and could also carry a pair of 66 or 132 lb (30 or 60 kg) bombs beneath the lower wings. During its early service on the China front it was frequently engaged in aerial combat or light bombing attacks, in addition to fulfilling its primary function, and scored a number of successes in engagements with opposing fighters. Production ended early in 1940, when seven hundred E8N aircraft had been built by Nakajima and an additional forty-eight by Kawanishi. Later production aircraft were powered by the 2-Kai-II version of the Kotobuki engine, with which they were designated E8N2. The Allied code name 'Dave' was given to the E8N after the outbreak of the Pacific war, during the early stages of which it continued to be used widely as a fleet co-operation aircraft, operating from battleships and cruisers of the IJN in the Aleutians and Philippines as well as from shore bases in the smaller island groups captured during the initial Japanese advances. After the Battle of Midway in June 1942 the E8N was gradually withdrawn from such duties to perform training or other secondary roles.

INDEX

The reference numbers refer to the illustrations and corresponding text.